Heidi Ellert-McDermott is a TV director/writer turned speechwriter. She worked at the BBC for the majority of her fifteen-year career, producing and directing entertainment shows. It was her love of comedy scriptwriting that led to her giving a bride speech that got more compliments than her dress. Realising there was an appetite for wedding speeches that are modern, witty and unshackled by tradition, she set up Speechy, a bespoke wedding speech company, employing TV scriptwriters and comedians to help couples around the world achieve their wedding speech goals. The team's passion for storytelling is revolutionising the wedding scene and Heidi's speech advice has been quoted everywhere from the *Observer* to the *Daily Mail*, and from *The Drew Barrymore Show* to the *New York Times*. She lives in the Cotswolds, England with her husband Roger and two children. And, yes, she did write Roger's groom speech.

The Modern Couple's Guide to Wedding Speeches

How to Write and Deliver an Unforgettable Speech or Toast

••

Heidi Ellert-McDermott

ROBINSON

ROBINSON

First published in Great Britain in 2023
by Robinson

10 9 8 7 6 5 4 3

Copyright © Heidi Ellert-McDermott,
2023

A CIP catalogue record for this book
is available from the British Library.

ISBN: 978-1-4721-4756-1

Typeset in Scala Sans and Sentinel
by Mousemat Design Limited
Printed and bound in Great Britain by
Clays Ltd, Elcograf S.p.A.

Papers used by Robinson are from
well-managed forests and other
responsible sources.

MIX
Paper from
responsible sources
FSC® C104740

Robinson
An imprint of
Little, Brown Book Group
Carmelite House
50 Victoria Embankment
London EC4Y 0DZ

An Hachette UK Company
www.hachette.co.uk

www.littlebrown.co.uk

How To Books are published by
Robinson, an imprint of Little,
Brown Book Group. We welcome
proposals from authors who have
first-hand experience of their
subjects. Please set out the aims
of your book, its target market and
its suggested contents in an email
to howto@littlebrown.co.uk.

To Roger, who was willing to marry me.

(Which gave me the opportunity to deliver a wedding speech, which inspired me to set up Speechy, which resulted in this publishing deal, which meant I haven't really spoken to him in about six months. Sorry about that.)

Contents

Introduction

WHY YOU NEED THIS BOOK

When it comes to wedding speeches, most people are novices so it's no surprise you need help. And even if you're a 'seasoned pro', this book can *still* help you improve on your previous effort(s).

While there's a lot of wedding speech advice out there, you may have already noticed that not all of it is good. Or even relevant.

Luckily, this book doesn't assume you're male, straight, have a questionable sense of humour or are incapable of having a unique thought. (Though, if that *is* the case, it will help you with at least two of those.)

This is a book designed for twenty-first-century couples – and not just the ones who met on Tinder! This book is for *any* couple who knows a great wedding speech is worth investing in; the 60-year-old ones, the childhood sweethearts (it happens), the traditional folk, the couples with two penises, the religious duos, the second-timers and the all-out weirdos.

The only assumptions this book makes are: 1) you're in love; and 2) you know that a wonderful wedding speech will add an awesome moment to your day.

So, wherever you live, whatever you believe in, however dysfunctional your family are, this book is designed to help you ditch the cheesy clichés, say no to internet gags and, instead, help you kick-start your marriage with a bang.

In fact, it's not just *your* speech I'm going to help with; this book is going to ensure *all* the speeches at your wedding are memorable.

And, crucially, for the *right* reasons.

MEET YOUR SPEECH STYLIST

I spent fifteen years of my life as a TV director, producer and writer before I decided to become a professional ghostwriter and specialise in love.

After witnessing some horrendous speeches (including two where the speaker was escorted away from the mic) and subsequently delivering my own bride speech, I knew there was a market for a more modern and better class of wedding speech.

I set up Speechy, the bespoke speechwriting business, in 2015 and recruited a crack team of TV and comedy writers to join me on my mission to make wedding speeches better. The team have written for BBC comedy shows, ghostwritten for high-profile comedians and are often panellists on topical entertainment shows. They're all expert storytellers and thoroughly decent folk.

Millions of people have now visited the Speechy site and, between us, we've helped thousands of couples around the world deliver their dream speech.

When Speechy first went online, I thought most of our clients would be despairing best men, but actually the vast majority of people contacting us were nearlyweds. And not just grooms needing a last-minute speech the day before the wedding (though there will always be a few of them!) but grooms, brides and couples getting in touch, sometimes a year in advance, because they wanted to deliver a truly beautiful and brilliant speech.

What I also realised is that not *everyone* contacting us needed their very own bespoke speechwriter. Some people just needed a kick-start, while some couples actually *wanted* to write their own speech but lacked the basic storytelling techniques to help them turn a good speech into something a little more wonderful.

I also noticed that 90 per cent of the first drafts emailed to us (as part of our Edit Service), suffered from similar issues. People kept making the same basic speechwriting mistakes and it became too frustrating *not* to write this book and tell you all.

And, so, here you are: the wedding speechwriter's guide to nailing your wedding speech.

WHY YOUR WEDDING SPEECH MATTERS

My first job is to get you excited about writing this speech because there's a rumour going round that it should be hard and painful.

It's not. Read this book and you'll 'get it'.

You may be 'linguistically challenged' today but by page 183 you'll be a professional storyteller. And let's face it, telling a story sounds more fun than writing a speech.

Storytelling is actually hardwired into our DNA. It's what connects us as humans. It's the essential glue that bonds people and helps us give meaning to our lives.

We're programmed through history to care about stories. In fact, gossip helped our ancestors survive. 'Pretty sure he's a Neanderthal. Don't swipe right.'

Today, storytelling is big business. It's at the heart of global marketing campaigns. It's a billion-dollar entertainment and publishing industry. It's at the root of political propaganda. Clearly, storytelling is powerful and important.

But when, exactly, do we have the opportunity to tell *our* story? When do we sum up what we're all about and why we love the things and people that we do?

Unless you're an Instagram influencer with cute hair, a cool backdrop and a quirky hashtag, the answer is rarely, if at all.

Isn't it a shame that so many of us leave it for *other* people to tell our story and explain our motivations in life, when we're lying there... dead. I mean, how ridiculous is that?

A wedding speech is essentially the yin to a eulogy's yang. It is just as important, just as moving and just as life-affirming, but – good news – you're around to enjoy it.

Your wedding speech is important, not just to you, but to the people you love. It's a once-in-a-lifetime opportunity to thank your parents and friends, and tell them why you love them. And it's one of the rare occasions when you can shout about how much you adore your partner without your mates sticking their fingers down their throats.

The flowers at a wedding might add beauty and the vows may add meaning, but the speeches? Well, they add the heart. They provide the day with its personality and show what 'you two' are all about.

Your guests may forget what they ate, they won't remember what they danced to but, as Maya Angelou reportedly said, 'people will never forget how you made them feel'.

HOW TO USE THIS BOOK

The book is written for a global audience. Straight or gay, whatever your religious views, wherever you live, you'll get something from this guide.

Speech traditions vary around the world. In fact, many couples don't even refer to them as speeches; they're wedding toasts. However, for the purpose of this book, we will refer to the full-length oration as the 'speech' and the final call to raise a glass as the 'toast'.

Meanwhile, some cultures are relative newcomers to the toast tradition, with speeches at Asian weddings really only becoming popular in the last few decades.

But whether you've sat through dozens of wedding speeches or hardly any, whether you're a natural storyteller or find it a struggle, this book is your ultimate ally and yours to play with.

It's been written to get you working from the get-go, so make sure you're ready to take notes and scribble as you go. Laptop, voice-notes, or old-school pen and paper – whatever works for you.

It's designed to be used as a couple but it's up to you whether you read it one after the other, fight over it chapter by chapter, or read it together. Whatever the case, planning and writing your speeches is more fun if you do it as a team.

(Of course, if your partner has absolutely no interest in the speeches and you're flying solo, enjoy the best bit of wedding planning there is and leave them to organise the day's transport.) So, how does this work?

Stage 1
First of all, we'll get you thinking about *all* the speeches at your wedding.

While you can't actually write the other speakers' speeches for them (this may seem ever so slightly controlling), you can do your best to ensure they're great.

We'll get you thinking about . . .

- Who you want to hear from on the day.
- How to schedule the speeches.
- How you can minimise the speech politics.

Next, it's time to decide how you'll represent your union on mic.

- Will it be one of you delivering a speech? And if so, how will you reflect your partner's thoughts and personality?
- Will both of you be giving a solo speech? And, if so, who should be thanking whom?
- Or would a joint speech work for you?

Stage 2
Now, it's about gathering your material.

I'll reveal all my wordsmithy tricks and techniques; you bring the stories, anecdotes and insights.

We'll cover . . .

- The modern speech etiquette rules and 'to dos'.

- Making your thank-yous meaningful.
- Paying tribute to your dearly departed friends or family.
- How to find strong stories and develop insightful observations.
- How to be funny without resorting to googled gags.
- Nailing the sentiment without being cheesy.

Stage 3
Next, you'll learn the tricks of the speechwriting trade so you can structure and write your speech.

Find out . . .

- How to curate your content.
- How to develop a narrative theme.
- How to structure your speech with an exciting opening, an engaging middle and an inspiring toast.
- How to write a joint or rhyming speech.
- How to edit your speech so it's punchy and powerful.

Stage 4
Finally, I'll take you through the presenting principles so you deliver your speech like a pro.

With over fifteen years of TV directing under my belt, I'll reveal how to . . .

- Rehearse effectively.
- Overcome nerves.
- Pace your speech.
- Use your body.
- Converse, rather than present.

Throughout the book, there's also examples of speeches the Speechy team have written so you can see the advice in action.

Some speeches are funnier, some are more sentimental. Some

I hope you love, some you might not.

I've purposely included a range of speech styles and the demographics of the (imaginary) couples delivering them are also varied. Older and younger, gay and straight, religious and atheist couples are featured, but even if the speaker's profile differs from yours, you can still learn something from every speech.

There's lots more inspiration dotted throughout the book too, so feel free to dive right in, steal the best lines and claim them as your own. But, first, give yourself the chance to discover you're actually rather good at this speechwriting malarkey.

Get scribbling, get silly and start speeching.

WHO'S WHO – MEET THE EXPERTS

I'll be quoting wedding influencers and writing experts throughout the book, so let me introduce you to them:

'Speeches can either make a wedding fly or drain it of all life.

'As a guest, I want to know where the love is. I want to learn something about the couple, either individually or as a duo, and I want to be left rooting for their marriage.

'Speeches have the power to surprise and delight, and a great speech creates the roadmap of the couple's relationship for the guests. It should help us understand where they've come from and how it relates to where they're going.'

EDUARDO BRANIFF, EDITOR-IN-CHIEF AT MEN'S VOWS

'Wedding speeches are increasingly being filmed so there's an added pressure and an added fear of getting it wrong. There's now even more expectation from the guests that the speeches will contain original content delivered in an original way.'

ALISON HARGREAVES, FOUNDER OF GUIDES FOR BRIDES

'A wedding speech is not something you can phone in. You have to "give it". And that involves work.

'If you want to connect with your guests, you need to avoid being generic. When you're giving a speech, the hardest thing to be is yourself but that's who your friends and family want to see.'

ALAN BERG, PUBLIC SPEAKING EXPERT AND ONE OF ONLY THIRTY-NINE GLOBAL SPEAKING FELLOWS IN THE WORLD

'I believe that a great toast can set the tone for the whole evening. The most memorable toasts I've heard over the years all create a sense of unity in the room; everyone is laughing, crying and the energy in the room is palpable.'

COLLEEN KENNEDY COHEN, CELEBRITY WEDDING PLANNER

'I'm a sucker for the speeches, even as a professional speechwriter. I'm always excited by the idea of them and yes, sometimes they can be disappointing, but people say the sorts of things in a wedding speech that they will never say in any other context.

'The emotion, the honesty, can be impactful.'

TOM COLES FROM 'ED AMSDEN AND TOM COLES', TV SCRIPTWRITING DUO AND PART OF THE SPEECHY TEAM

'Couples are not making the most of their wedding speeches. In fact, a lot of couples don't say a word at their wedding because people just don't want to do it!

'Speeches should never take time away from the dancefloor, but they should project a level of gratitude and emotion with a celebratory approach.'

DAVID TUTERA, CELEBRITY WEDDING & EVENT PLANNER

'A couple of decades ago, the majority of speeches at South Asian weddings were awful; far too long and parents showing off about their children's achievements. Thankfully, things have changed.

'The scene has finally caught up with the potential of speeches to add humour and emotion to the day and I now see the speeches are a wedding day highlight. Most of the time at least!'
SHAI HUSSAIN, SPEECHY WEDDING SPEECHWRITER AND COMEDY WRITER

'Almost all other elements of the wedding have become more bespoke, with couples opting to do things "their way" but speeches are the last thing to be revolutionised. It frustrates me how old fashioned most wedding speech line-ups still are.

'I'd like to see more nearlyweds investing time in their speeches. They're a chance to celebrate the person who means the most to you in the world and a rare opportunity to tell all the people you love how cool you think they are.'
ZOE BURKE, EDITOR AT HITCHED; THE KNOT WORLDWIDE

'When I got married in 2008, I really struggled to find alternative wedding inspiration, or sources of cool and different ideas, so I didn't even really consider the speeches and who would be giving them. We just did the traditional ones (groom, father of the bride, best man).

'It's great that that's changed. These days, I would definitely give a bride speech. Sometimes people need a kick-start to start thinking a bit differently.'
KAT WILLIAMS, FOUNDER OF ROCK N ROLL BRIDE

'Without the speeches, you have the meal, the ceremony, photos and disco but you don't get much opportunity to speak to the couple yourself. Sometimes you never do!

'Speeches make sure the couple speaks to everyone in a non-religious and genuine way. They're crucial in making sure everyone feels connected to the newlyweds.'

CLAIRE WETTON, SPEECHY WEDDING SPEECHWRITER AND TV SCRIPTWRITER

'Speeches can definitely be seen as a drag but in my opinion, they can be one of the best and most touching parts of a wedding.

'Weddings can be busy, overwhelming affairs so speeches give everyone a chance to take a moment to sit back and focus on the couple they're celebrating for a few moments.'

HAMISH SHEPHARD, FOUNDER OF BRIDEBOOK

'I think delivering wedding speeches is a practice being adopted in more international cultures and it's becoming a trend around the world. People are seeing more videos of funny and emotional speeches on social media and TV shows and they're catching on to the joy of them.'

ELEONORA TUCCI, GROUP EDITOR AT WEDDINGS & HONEYMOONS MEDIA

'After the pandemic, the wedding rules relaxed and couples' priorities changed. The vibe now is more bespoke and couples are paying closer attention to their speeches and many more are delivering personalised, handwritten vows too.'

ANNA PRICE OLSON, WEDDING EXPERT, EDITOR AT BRIDES FOR MORE THAN EIGHT YEARS

'Speeches are arguably the most personal reminder and memento from the day.

'It's something that will echo through your friendships and relationships for the years to come. It can be daunting but it's also an incredible opportunity.'

ANDREW SHANAHAN, SPEECHY WEDDING SPEECHWRITER
AND JOURNALIST

'All I know is my wedding speech was one of the favourite parts of my wedding day. I made my friends laugh and I ensured everyone I love felt vital to the day and a little more cherished.

'I was glad my groom got a few compliments thrown his way and to publicly confess how much I love him. Trust me, I don't do that often.

'In the end, my bride speech got more compliments than my dress. And I actually think that's rather wonderful.'

ME

Stage 1 – Plan Your Speeches

Over the last couple of decades, weddings have changed immeasurably. A couple's nuptials are now expected to be a representation of them and *say* something about who they are.

And yet, ironically, wedding speakers have been saying pretty much the same thing for far too long.

The plan

In this chapter, we'll cover ...

- Creative ways to **schedule your speeches.**
- How to curate your **wedding speech line-up.**
- **How to handle the inevitable speech politics** of asking certain people to speak but not others.
- **Useful information to give your speakers.**
- **How you two will represent yourselves on the day** – one speech, two speeches or a joint speech?
- **Stage management** – the tech, the equipment and the Master of Ceremonies.

SCHEDULING YOUR SPEECHES

Guess what? Your wedding speeches don't need to be limited to three and they don't need to be allocated to a 'speech clump' time zone. In fact, we'd go so far as to say, your speeches *shouldn't* come packaged to bore.

Think big but not lengthy. No one wants to sit through a solid hour of speeches unless you have Ricky Gervais as your best man or Melissa McCarthy is your mum.

Scheduling options

In the US, speeches are just as common at the rehearsal dinner (the formal dinner prior to the wedding that the 'top table' are invited to) as on the wedding day itself.

Meanwhile, in Scandinavian countries, there is often an invite for everyone to propose a toast *at any point* during the wedding dinner (we'll go into this in more detail on page 16).

At many British weddings, the speeches are scheduled *before* the wedding meal; the idea is that everyone is officially welcomed to the wedding and the speakers are quickly able to relax (and tuck into the free wine!).

Of course, some couples opt for speeches *after* the wedding meal (or before the dessert), once everyone has eaten and had a chance to chat and drink. As a speaker, there's certainly something to be said for your guests having had a bit of laughter-lubricant. Equally, you may find people are more likely to be rowdy so be prepared for some good-natured heckling.

An increasingly popular idea is separating your speeches so they're spread *between* courses. This works particularly well if you're having more than three speakers.

For example ...

- Master of Ceremonies (MC) welcomes guests and introduces first speaker.
- Father of the bride (5 minutes).
- **Starter.**
- **Main course.**
- MC welcomes second speaker.
- Mother of the groom (5 minutes).
- MC welcomes third speaker.
- Maid of honour (7 minutes).
- **Dessert.**
- MC welcomes fourth speakers.

- The joint couple speech (9 minutes).
- MC welcomes fifth speaker.
- Best man (7 minutes).

Of course, if you're having a wedding weekend, you have more time to play with . . .

- **Rehearsal dinner** – 2 speakers.
- **Prior to the wedding-day meal** – Spousal speech plus 2 speakers.
- **After the meal / During dessert** – Everyone invited to propose a toast.

The benefit of having the speeches spaced out is that there's less chance of the guests getting bored with the stand up, sit down routine of too many toasts one after the other. It's also less likely that the speeches feel repetitive or overly lengthy.

However, as Zoe Burke points out, wedding photographers and catering staff can struggle with spread-out speeches as they make the day's timings complicated: 'I put a post out encouraging our Hitched nearlyweds to consider scheduling their speeches a bit differently and I got loads of DMs back from venues and photographers saying, please, stop recommending it! I'm still a fan but couples should definitely brief their suppliers in advance of the day so they're fully prepared for the challenge.'

From personal experience, I know it's possible to schedule speeches between courses, but it's important to give realistic estimates of the speech duration. Here's what some of the influencers had to say about scheduling . . .

'I like when the speeches come after the main course and before dessert as it means no one is left starving for too long.

'I remember going to a wedding where the speeches were before

the food. Unfortunately, the speeches went on for an hour and a quarter, and what was even worse is I could smell the beef Wellington getting slowly killed in the kitchen. By the time it was served, everyone was famished and hammered, and the meal was close to ruined.

'The same speeches, delivered after the main course, would have been well received by the guests . . . and the chef!'

ALISON HARGREAVES

'The newlyweds might actually give a couple of speeches over the course of the celebration.

The speeches at the rehearsal dinner are generally always great as it's a more intimate audience that knows the couple extremely well. Speeches on the wedding day might feel very different.'

ANNA PRICE OLSON

Ultimately, there's no right and wrong. I'm a big fan of breaking up the speeches but not everyone agrees, so the scheduling of your speeches really is yours to play with (and we'll cover the pros and cons of each option on page 18).

Scandi-speeches

One way to shake up the scheduling debate is to invite everyone who fancies it to stand up, clink their glass and give an 'ad hoc' toast during the meal or between courses.

You can suggest the idea in your invites and get the MC to remind guests of this opportunity prior to sitting down.

The benefit is, not only is it fun to get everyone involved, it also takes the pressure off the 'main' speakers.

Of course, you may *still* want to get proper, loving tributes from your family and some hardcore roastings from your mates, but this idea allows your naughty cousin to get involved, as well as your lovely boss and your twelve-year-old nephew.

It basically ensures you have a solid couple of hours of people throwing massive compliments and love-bombs in your direction and, really, who can argue with that?

Well...

...the *possible* downside is that people have too much to drink, speakers babble on for far too long and it all descends into chaos. That's fine if you're cool with that but make sure the important people get heard too.

Prep anyone *not* on the metaphoric 'top table' to keep their toasts to less than two minutes and make sure your MC is assertive enough to call time on anyone who goes on too long.

Eduardo Braniff is a fan: 'The concept gives guests who are moved the opportunity to express it. And I always love the little glimmers of truth that get divulged along the way.

'Get a good MC moderating so there remains a sense of control. You need someone assertive and witty enough to bring a rambling toast to a conclusion.'

Alison Hargreaves is less of a fan. 'Spontaneous speeches are a good idea for second marriages when couples want to move on from the traditional speeches but the downside is people often feel obliged to say something when they don't actually have that much to say. It can become very repetitive.'

Personally, I've been to a couple of weddings where the idea has worked really well. It's obviously more suited to the boho, relaxed wedding vibe as opposed to a formal affair.

If you fancy it, here's how you can invite your guests to get involved.

Scheduling recap

So what do you two think?

In a recent online poll for Guides for Brides, 74 per cent of respondents said they preferred the speeches delivered in one hit but think about what works best for the day you have planned.

	Pros	Cons
Before dinner	• Immediately welcomes your guests to the day • There's something for guests to talk about and bond over straight away • Speakers can relax • Easy to co-ordinate	• Guests haven't settled into the day. They're still on their best behaviour and sober • Speeches one after the other can become boring, especially if there are a lot of toasts or repetition • Guests may become hungry • The duration of each speech will have to be kept tight to ensure the caterers can cope • It limits the number of speakers (as you wouldn't want too many one after the other)

After the main course	• Easy to co-ordinate • Guests are relaxed and have had a drink (cue more laughter) • Guests won't be hungry	• Speakers can't relax till after dinner • Speeches one after the other can be boring • People may be keen to get to the bar or dancefloor • It limits the number of speakers
Spaced-out speeches	• Each speech is given its own time to shine • You can have more speakers on your line-up • Each speech can be slightly longer than if it was delivered alongside others • Less danger of the speeches feeling too long or boring • Can schedule the nervous speakers earlier and the funnier ones later in the day	• Harder to co-ordinate • The first speaker is more likely to be addressing guests who have not quite relaxed into the day – i.e. a tougher crowd • The final speakers might not be able to relax through the meal (or could be in danger of becoming *too* relaxed!)
Scandi-style	• Less pressure on each speaker • Couples get to hear from more of their friends and family (depending on your family, this may also be a con!) • Adds a sense of fun	• Less control over who speaks or what is said • Can get rowdy!

YOUR SPEECH LINE-UP

Okay, we've got the scheduling sorted, now who's part of the line-up?

Well, I'm glad you've asked, because so many couples *don't*!

The shade of confetti gets debated, the words on the chalkboard get a good five minutes and even the favours demand a conversation – but the speech line-up, something that all the guests will focus on for a good chunk of the wedding, well, that's just *assumed* most of the time, isn't it?

At straight weddings it's the father of the bride, groom, and best man. Doesn't matter if the best man is a liability or if the dad hates public speaking – rules are rules.

But here's the thing: there are *no* rules.

Same-sex weddings are one step ahead here and aren't shackled to the usual format. But every couple, straight or gay, should spend time discussing their speech line-up *together* before anyone assumes they'll be given mic time.

Today, I estimate less than 50 per cent of weddings have the old-school father of the bride, groom and best man option, so who's taking their place?

Well, obviously, more women, in every role, from brides and bridesmaids to sisters and mums. Also, uncles of the bride, and mothers and fathers of the groom. Grandparents occasionally. And children too. Adult, teenage and even younger.

The demographic of Speechy's clientele is diverse and changing every year to reflect the age and values we live in. Yes, there's still tradition to consider and, to be fair, that deserves *some* thought, but so do lots of other things:

- Who do you genuinely want to hear from on the day?
- How many speeches do you want in total?
- Who has lots to say and would love to give a speech?
- Who can be relied upon to deliver an entertaining, funny speech?

- Who can deliver the poignant one?
- Will anyone be annoyed if they're *not* asked? (Sadly, not something to be overlooked.)
- Do you have any women on the mic?

Overload, anyone? Okay, let's go through it step by step.

Speech politics

Before we get to *your* dream line-up, let's acknowledge the speech politics involved.

Wouldn't it be wonderful if all your friends and family were delighted to be asked to speak and relieved if they weren't?

Well, that's as likely as a venue offering a 'wedding discount'.

Take your dad for example. He might be disappointed if he isn't asked to speak, even if he's not the most eloquent of characters or despite the fact his style of humour verges on the Les Dawson. (Google him. Not good.)

If you *do* have a potentially dull or renegade speaker, whether it's your dad or a best mate, then do your best to help them out. Firstly, check they actually *want* to give a speech. Believe it or not, they may not want to dust down their best Les Dawson impression for public consumption.

If they *do* expect some mic time, make sure you give them clear guidance. By this, we don't mean threatening them or 'kindly' buying them a speech template but rather giving them some basic parameters (see page 27) and requesting a short duration.

Remind any speakers that they *can* get help. Tell your dad to get your mum or siblings involved; he is, after all, representing the whole family.

If your parents are divorced and there are close step-parents involved too, it can be hard to nominate just one of them to speak. Sometimes it makes sense to have two speakers (for example, your mum *and* dad giving separate speeches at different points of the day), but you don't want your speech line-up to be designed purely to keep everyone *else* happy.

THE DISTRACTION TECHNIQUE

One way to mitigate against the speech politics is to give people *another* job.

For example, can your stepdad be a witness or give a reading? Or can your renegade mate be in charge of the stag or hen do (bachelor party or bridal shower) rather than the speech? Maybe it's sensible to put Mad Pete in charge of the rings and Sensible Sam on speech-duty. The MC role is also an important job but one where you can't go too wrong.

Ultimately, everyone *should* understand this is 'your day' (cliché klaxon) but sometimes that's not the reality of the situation. Sometimes we just have to do the best we can with the nutty folk we love.

As much as the speeches have the power to add something marvellous to your day, they certainly shouldn't add additional stress. Don't start thinking they need to be Oscar-worthy and don't feel you're responsible for the words coming out of other people's mouths.

On the day, you just need to sit back and hope people say nice things about you.

Line up, line up

Now we've sorted the politics, who exactly do you *want* to hear from on the day?

Zoe Burke suggests you ask yourself, 'If I didn't know anything about wedding traditions, who would I ask to speak?'

As a guide, you generally need...

- Someone (friend or family) paying a tribute to Spouse 1.
- Someone (friend or family) paying a tribute to Spouse 2.
- Someone representing the newly hitched (Spouse 1, Spouse 2 or both of you).

As we know, at straight weddings, this has traditionally meant: father of the bride, groom and best man. Sometimes, it's appropriate to stick to this line-up but not as often as it occurs.

So, let's consider who you might want in that line-up instead, or even in addition to.

THE BRIDE (IF YOU HAVE ONE)

At straight weddings, brides are a remarkably underutilised resource on the day.

Obviously, brides shouldn't feel pressured to do *anything* they don't fancy at their wedding, and if public speaking isn't your thing, then fine, don't do it. But, at least, spend five minutes *thinking* about doing it.

From personal experience, I can highly recommend it.

For a start, you get to thank all your favourite people rather than your partner speaking 'on behalf' of you. You also get to pay tribute to the person you just married which seems only fair. And, giving a speech is actually great fun if you know you're delivering a good 'un.

Delivering my bride speech was, without a doubt, one of the highlights of my day. Far more emotional and meaningful than the vows (sorry vicar).

In a survey by Bridebook, 42 per cent of brides said they planned to make a speech at their wedding. Bridebook founder Hamish Shephard is passionate about the subject:

'Back in 2018, I actually wrote an open letter to all our brides, encouraging them to make a speech at their wedding. I'd just attended my great friend Katie's wedding and been blown away by the heartfelt speech she gave. It provoked a huge discussion at the wedding about why it was so rare to hear a bride's speech and many recently married brides were suddenly frustrated that they hadn't given one themselves!

'Since then, I've definitely seen more and more women

stepping up to the mic, whether that's brides, mums or maids of honour. In couples made up of a bride and groom especially, it's fantastic to see them start their marriage with equal voices.

'Of course, there's still room for change and I'll always continue to encourage more women to take the mic. Actually, something I'd personally love to see become more common is speeches from the mums.'

Talking of which . . .

OTHER WOMEN

Whether or not a bride speech is on the itinerary, make sure you consider the other brilliant women on your guestlist who could step up to the mic.

In an online poll for Guides for Brides, 62 per cent of people said they disliked male-only wedding speech line-ups, so it's your duty to have a think. Obviously this pressure may not apply to gay unions but you don't get a completely free pass.

Surely we can all appreciate what our mums have to say? Perhaps as a joint mum and dad speech, an idea I'm seeing put into practice more and more.

Maybe the best woman could give a great speech? Or what about the groom's sister? Siblings always have a lot of ammunition up their sleeves (even if it *is* a sleeveless Carolina Herrera number).

As Zoe Burke adds, 'We're seeing more brides, mums and bridesmaids giving speeches but not enough.

'All the other aspects of the wedding seem to be evolving, with more mums walking their daughters down the aisle or best women being in charge of the rings, but speeches aren't being considered as much.'

Make sure you do!

THE QUIRKY CURVEBALLS

Don't just go for the obvious. If you want to charm the pants off your guests, look at the youngsters and oldies you have to play with.

The grandmas and grandpas in the room; doesn't really matter what they say, they're guaranteed to get folk smiling.

Ask them to read out a funny poem or just a couple of (comedy) lines offering you their very personal marriage advice. Often this can be on the cheeky side (result!) or sometimes, it can offer a real insight into how timeless love really is (hankies at the ready).

And then we have the young 'uns. This works especially well if you or your partner already have children but godsons, nieces, any little tyke really, can be entertaining.

Tailor their input depending on their age. Teenagers often love writing their own speeches but they have the potential to waffle. Limit them to a 400-word count and encourage them to test it out on an adult before the actual day.

If your niece is a huge Harry Potter fan, challenge her to give you some poignant marriage advice using only Hogwarts quotes. Or get your seven-year-old godson to give you his top five ways to show someone you love them.

Even pre-school children can get involved if you plan it well. Get them to hold up comedy signs at suitable points throughout your speech (for example, 'Not true', 'They're exaggerating', 'Don't believe a word').

There's nothing better than a four-year-old heckler to get people laughing.

GUEST INPUT AND SPEECH CASTING (IF YOU DARE!)

Eduardo Braniff had an innovative (slightly controversial) idea when I was chatting to him:

'One idea I'd like to see become more common is for couples to ask people to send in their speeches in advance of the wedding and then the couple decide on the three they'd like to include as part of the day.

'Obviously, the choice would have to be tactfully relayed back to everyone. Maybe the couple could print all the speeches and display them in a book for everyone to read at the reception to make sure all their thoughts and sentiment were genuinely appreciated.'

While I take a perverse pleasure in this idea ('Mate, would you like to audition to be part of the speech line-up?') the reality of keeping potential speakers on-side might be too much for the majority of us to handle.

Getting everyone's input is a great idea though and it's something I did at my wedding. In our invites we asked everyone to send us their favourite piece of marriage advice along with their RSVP.

Not only did we love reading the advice as it came in, we selected our favourites to read as part of my husband's speech.

The advice varied from thoughtful quotes by romantic poets to original, humorous advice from mates.

Our favourite marriage tip was 'no number twos in front of each other', something that has kept our marriage strong to this day.

Here's how to get the best from your guests; either in the old-school invites or as part of your wedding website.

WE NEED YOUR MARRIAGE ADVICE!

In advance of the wedding day, we'd love to hear your best pieces of marriage advice so we can get swotting up and share some of your wisest (and funniest) tips with the rest of our guests on the day.

We welcome any advice you can give us – from the profound to the perverse, from the sentimental to the silly. We'd love to hear your original observations or even just clever quotes you've stolen from other people.

Email over your marriage advice or add it to the RSVP within the next fortnight!

Line-up recap

Possible speakers	
The traditional three	Do you think they'd want to give a speech? Do *you* want them to give a speech? If not, refer to speech politics and the distraction technique on page 22.
Women	Have you got this covered?
The older generation	Anyone worth considering?
The younger generation	Anyone worth considering?
Someone who's likely to be funny	Have you got this covered?
Someone who's likely to be poignant	Have you got this covered?

It's unlikely you'll tick every box and not every element is essential. You do not *need* a young person or an older person as part of the line-up; it's simply something to consider.

SPEECH THERAPY – ADVICE FOR SPEAKERS

Okay, now the line-up is sorted, it's time to help your speakers out.

Consider yourself their speech therapist. It's your job to help all your speakers feel confident, comfortable and excited about giving their speech.

People don't give wedding speeches very often so most folk appreciate a guiding hand. This is the sort of info that's helpful without seeming too controlling.

- **Introduction** – Do they need to introduce themselves or will there be an MC on the day?
- **Mic** – Will they be expected to use one?
- **Expected duration** – All speeches should be under ten minutes long. It seems obvious but we've seen several speeches (generally the best men) go well over half an hour, oblivious to the yawns or heckling.

    There really is **no minimum length.** A speaker can say a lot in just a few sentences but that takes a lot of skill. Suggesting your main speakers deliver a speech of three minutes or less is a bit tight.

    Rather than talking about the length of the speech, it's often easier to talk in terms of word count. We'd suggest recommending **between 750 and 1,300 words** depending on how many speeches you're planning on the day and who the speaker is. As a basic guide, people can usually deliver **about 150 words per minute**, not allowing for pauses or laughter.
- **Any 'to dos'** – Is there anything you'd like them to include within their speech? Are there any practicalities relating to the day or maybe you'd like them to propose the toast to the dearly departed.
- **Anything specific to avoid** – Yes, sometimes it's worth mentioning you'd prefer *not* to be reminded about your exes on your wedding day and make sure your father knows not to mention your childhood nickname in front of your boss.
- **Language** – Sometimes friends haven't considered if children will be at the wedding (or they just don't care). If you do, make sure you brief your speakers about what's appropriate. I generally say that b-words are the profanity limit (as most parents will know that a few 'bloody bollocks' may be dropped when the best man takes the mic) but this is something you have to gauge depending on your guestlist.

- **Behaviour** – It would be nice to assume that everyone you invite to speak considers it an honour and tries their best to do you proud but we've seen some speakers (the best mates again) who see it as an opportunity to get pissed and put on an embarrassing show.

  A gentle reminder to the best man/woman about the range of guests at the wedding ('Great Aunty Betty's coming!') will hopefully be enough of a warning without turning the 'honour' of speaking turning into a begrudging obligation.
- **Who to toast** – Despite all the online etiquette guides, speakers still get confused about who they should toast. It's good practice to help people out so not everyone is proposing a toast to the bridesmaids.

Of course, think about how to present this info. Get it wrong and it could easily be interpreted as demanding and over-the-top, so put away the PowerPoint, the capital letters or the request for anyone to sign a non-disclosure agreement. Just have a casual chat and email them any specific points if they show an interest.

As Alison Hargreaves says, 'Generally, people will be thankful if you suggest a short duration for their speech. And some people really have no idea how long they should be, it seems a lot of people imagine they need to be twenty minutes!

'I once went to a wedding where there were two best men delivering separate speeches. Unfortunately, their experiences with the groom were very similar and they told almost identical stories.

'This is why the couple should make it clear to all the speakers what their role is on the line-up and ensure there isn't any duplication.

'Couples should treat their speeches as one overall performance. You wouldn't start a play until you knew who was covering which part of the script.'

Here's an example of a note you could send to your speakers in advance of the day.

Speech-notes for speakers

Hello – thank you for accepting the dubious honour of giving a speech at our wedding.

We know this may have put you into a panic so here's some basic information in case you don't have a clue.

- **Intro** – You will / won't be introduced by an MC so you don't need / you will need to introduce yourself.
- **Etiquette** – The first speaker can welcome everyone to the wedding but no one needs to thank anyone specific for coming. That's our job so you can relax.
- **Suggested duration** – that's about (*you decide*) words. Obviously we won't be timing you but if you start getting heckled you know why ;-)
- **Equipment** – There will / won't be a mic so you might want to / there's no need to practise on a hairbrush.
- **Kids** – There will / won't be children present so feel free to be your normal self / resist the urge to be too sweary.
- **Your fellow speakers** – The other speakers at the wedding will be (*TBC*). Feel free to outdo us all with your comedy genius and profound sentiment!
- **Your toast** – So you don't overlap with the other speakers – please can you direct your toast to (*you decide*).

Finally, feel free to delete this immediately and do your own thing. We can't wait to hear your speech on the day!

Warning: despite all this effort, people can still go freestyle and do their own thing.

Resist the urge to rugby tackle them off the mic if they do.

YOUR SPEECH

So we've worked out who *else* will be speaking at your wedding, but what about you two?

If you've bought this book, we suspect at least one of you fancies giving a speech. (Or maybe one of you is subtly hinting the other better start thinking about it sharpish?)

Before making any decisions, let's look at the options . . .

One of you

The old-school choice.

It's worked for a fair few decades and it's a decent option if one of you hates the thought of giving a speech.

Of course, if you're in a straight union, let's *not* assume it's the bloke who's on speech-duty. The groom has an equal claim to a fear of public speaking.

If you do opt for the solo speech, this doesn't mean the other one can't have a say in it. It is, after all, representing *both* of you.

Speeches no longer have to be written in secret and rehearsed in a cupboard. In fact, they're generally better if they're not.

Two heads really are better than one.

Sure, keep a section of the speech (the romantic bit) to reveal on the day but otherwise, you have the ultimate editor by your side so why not exploit them?

Two-spouse speeches

If you've decided you both want to deliver a speech (generally more common in same-sex unions but growing in popularity across the board) then we advise *discussing* them.

Controversial, I know.

Yes, keep the romantic bits secret but you don't want the second speaker needlessly repeating the first or just being left with the speech-scraps.

Negotiate who gets to tell the story of how you got together and who gets to recount the anecdote about you accidentally getting locked in that bar one night (or was that just me?).

With the thank-yous it should be relatively easy to divvy them up; you'll probably *both* want to thank each set of parents but it makes sense for each of you to thank your own set of mates. For example, a groom doesn't need to toast the bridesmaids if the bride is giving a heartfelt thank-you herself.

Eduardo adds, 'If two grooms are each giving a speech, they need to discuss them to make sure they're not overlapping and each speech complements the other. Even better, get an outside editor, a trusted friend, to oversee the speeches for you!'

The joint speech

Whether it's a bride and groom or a same-sex wedding speech, joint speeches are a wedding trend that's set to stay. It's a great way of saying, 'BOOM, we're a team.'

You *both* get to thank your friends and family and you can rehearse your speech together.

It also takes the pressure off just one of you and allows you to discuss your speech and have fun with it along the way.

David Tutera said, 'Joey and I did it together! We went on the dance floor and went back and forth between us and it was great. We showed our abundance of love for the people that we wanted to be there and to me, that is the most important aspect of speeches.'

Many of our Speechy clients have said their joint speech became the epicentre of their day and every joint speech we've written has gone down a storm. They're unusual, they're modern and they're just really entertaining.

'A couple of decades ago couples started to care about the first dance and really turning that into something special, often taking professional dance lessons in advance. Now I think it's

time for the speeches to shine and for couples to wake up to how they can make them special too.'

ELEONORA TUCCI

'One trend I've loved seeing take off over the last few years is joint speeches from couples. It's a great way to kick off your marriage as a real unit.'

HAMISH SHEPHARD

Your speech recap

	Pros	Cons
Solo	• Best option if one of you hates public speaking • Speech time is kept short	• One of you speaks on behalf of the other • Guests miss hearing from both of you
2 Speeches	• You both get to say your piece	• The speeches may overlap (though you can mitigate this) • Increased length of speech-time • Negotiation over your best stories
Joint Speech	• A standout moment • Modern • You both have your say • Teamwork in action • No need to double up on the thank-yous • You both get to tell your best stories	• Harder to write • More rehearsal required

STAGE MANAGEMENT

MC or not MC?

Well, actually that's not much of a question. Even if you're only having three speakers, recruiting a Master of Ceremonies will help the speeches run smoothly.

The MC's job is simply to welcome everyone and introduce each speaker, meaning that no one has to intro themselves (well, other than the MC, ironically).

In terms of selecting the MC, it helps if they know at least a couple of the speakers and they're relatively witty.

If they don't personally know your cousin who's third on the line-up, make sure they're prepped with some background or even just give them a comedic line to introduce them.

Again, be clear about how long you expect them to talk (45-sec introduction and 30 seconds between each speaker is all that's required) and what exactly they need to do (for example, do they also have to announce the cutting of the cake?).

Equipment and tech

Luckily most weddings are now mic'd up. A decade ago I was going to weddings and couldn't hear half the speeches.

Wireless handheld mics and loudspeakers are now easy to source and there's plenty of sound specialists you can discuss your audio needs with.

Ideally, practise with your sound system in advance to develop good microphone etiquette. When you speak into a handheld mic, you generally want to hold it about 15–20 cm from your mouth to avoid 'popping'. And, once you find the right position, remember it!

As Alan Berg says, 'Novice speakers have a habit of forgetting the mic half way through their speech and dropping it down so their voice is no longer picked up. Or they get too expressive and start using the mic to anoint their audience like a priest would.'

If you don't want the hassle of holding a mic, consider using radio mics or invisible headsets. Radio mics (the ones that clip on to your clothes) can be hard to position on a bride's dress and you have to be conscious of not moving your head round too much. You obviously don't have that problem with wireless over-the-ear set mics but they do look a bit 'corporate'.

If you opt for radio or headset mics, you may then need to invest in a sound engineer to help fit and transfer them to the other speakers on the day.

Make sure your other speakers are briefed on what mic they will be using (and how they work) in advance.

And finally, with any tech you're planning on using, get someone to test it on the morning of the wedding so there are no unexpected glitches.

Positioning

Think about where each speaker will stand when they deliver their speech.

If it's a small to average-sized wedding, people can simply stand and deliver from where they're sat. If that's the plan, make sure they're seated somewhere where they can face all the guests and consider the logistics of using the mics if the speakers are not sat beside each other.

At larger weddings, you may want to ask speakers to deliver from a good viewing point. If so, consider investing in a lectern so speakers can use it for their notes. Source one that is unobtrusive and doesn't hide the speaker's body. Music stands work well and can be decorated according to your wedding theme.

When it comes to *your* speech, make sure you're near each other so you can interact throughout. As well as listening to your speech, your guests want to see your partner reacting to it.

Show you're a team: reassuring shoulder rubs, eye contact, pats on the back and a kiss at the end.

Stage management recap

- Select a 'safe pair of hands' to the MC role.
- Brief them on what is expected of them and who the speakers they will be introducing are.
- Ensure everyone will be able to *hear* the speakers and comfortably *see* them too. Ideally they also want to see you both throughout the speeches to see your reaction to them!

Stage 1 recap

Scheduling

- Decide on the style of your speeches; ad hoc and spontaneous, or scripted and considered.
- Schedule your speeches to complement the day. Consider before, during or after the meal. Give your speeches the opportunity to become the epicentre of your day.

Line-up

- Don't follow sexist or old-fashioned traditions without questioning them.
- Decide who you want to hear from and look at the overall demographic of your line-up.
- Think about the likely content of the speeches. Will there be sentimental and humorous moments?
- Give guidance to your speakers regarding duration and expectations.
- Finally, decide how you two will represent yourselves on the mic – one speech, two speeches or a joint speech.

Stage management

- Source a mic and sound system.
- Plan where the speakers will deliver from.

- Recruit an MC. Brief them about their role, their expected duration and the speakers they'll be introducing.

SPEECH INSPIRATION

Groom speech – Delivered by Ryan
Background: Ryan has married Misty. They live in Edinburgh, Scotland, and met through friends. Ryan's mum has passed away.

Good afternoon ladies and gentlemen, and welcome to what can only be described as the greatest day of my life. Well, *second* greatest day of my life, if you include the day Misty managed to not leave a wet towel on the bed. *(Pretend to wipe tear away)* Sorry, it's an emotional memory.

Firstly, on behalf of both Misty and me, let me thank you all for coming. I know many of you have travelled long distances to be here. And a special thanks to our English friends, many of whom see travelling north of the border as akin to entering the Squid Game. Your bravery is greatly appreciated.

Now, another person I'd like to thank is our mutual friend Lou who actually set us up six years ago. I mean, I say 'set up', she described me to Misty as 'average looking, but has nice shoes'.

But, uncharitable review or not, it certainly seemed to do the trick. When we met for the first time at Lou's birthday drinks, we immediately gravitated towards each other. We talked intensely all evening. It was one of those conversations where you lose all track of time and everything else just seems to drift into the background. We talked about life, hobbies, future plans and how when she was a kid, she was obsessed with Winnie the Pooh. Which makes it not at all surprising that she'd end up with me: a chubby character with one shirt and an aggressive appetite.

I remember coming away from that evening in a bit of a haze; not only had I found someone I liked, and who liked me back, but I'd also found someone who could still rap all the words to Eminem's 'Stan'.

I thought life couldn't get any better until, as we went to leave, she nervously turned to me and uttered those three magic words all guys want to hear: 'Fancy a kebab?'

It was then I knew I was in love.

It's a weird feeling meeting someone that you *know* you'd happily spend the rest of your life with. Before meeting Misty 'love' felt like just a word, and all of a sudden, she comes along and fills that word with meaning.

To this day, I've always maintained that it feels like we are two halves of the same whole. It felt like that then, and still does now, that we were just the right amount of similar, and just the right amount of different to be perfect together.

We complement each other's good traits, and soften each other's bad ones. By which I mean, I occasionally pick up her wet towels and she does literally everything else.

But I also mean that she has taught me a lot. She's taught me that kindness always wins, she's taught me that it's not the words you say, but the way you make people feel that gets remembered, and she's taught me that Marmite and cheese on crumpets is the greatest snack known to man.

She is the other side to my coin, the cheerful Winnie the Pooh to my grumpy Eeyore. And now, incredibly, she's my wife.

If you'll all allow me, I'd like to take this opportunity to mention some incredibly important people who have helped us not just today, but throughout our lives.

Firstly, I'd like to thank my dad, who has taught me that being a man isn't about machismo and bravado, it's about being warm, welcoming and caring. I've often been called a 'mini David', and it's something I'll continue to wear as a badge of honour.

To Misty's parents, June and Martin: your help with the

wedding planning has been utterly invaluable, and I can't thank you enough for how you've both welcomed me into your family. I'll look forward to many more Sunday dinners that end with Martin saying 'I'll get the whisky'.

To my groomsmen, for turning up both fully dressed and mostly sober, and also for years of support, advice and knowing exactly when I need a chat and a game of FIFA.

To Misty's bridesmaids for being amazing friends and helping everyone keep a cool head with yesterday's dress disaster. Your sage advice and support has always been a great comfort to Misty and me both.

And finally, I'd like to say thank you to a very special woman who is sadly no longer with us: my mum. There's no other way to say it, other than it's heartbreaking that she can't be here today. She was a person who was born to be at big events. A person who filled the room with her smile and her presence. And while she can't be with us, I know how much she approved of Misty, because in the latter weeks of her life, she tapped me on the hand and gently said, 'Misty is a keeper'.

So, Mum, I love you and I miss you, and I hope you're looking down on us today with your characteristic big smile on your face, safe in the knowledge that I've taken your advice on board.

Now, I'm not one for massive promises and grand gestures, but now seems like as good a moment as any to break from that tradition. So Misty, before I end this speech, I'd like to give you three promises for our future life together: I promise whenever you say 'Fancy a kebab?' I'll always say yes. I promise to always back you up by singing the Dido chorus in 'Stan', and I promise that no matter what, I'll spend the rest of my days attempting to make you as happy as you've made me.

So, without further ado, if you'll all kindly be upstanding, and join me in a toast to my best friend and love of my life: The new ... Mrs Misty Ferguson! (*Raise toast*)

WRITTEN BY ED AMSDEN AND TOM COLES

ZAC: Hello and thanks to everyone for joining us today.

HOLLY: For those of you who know us well, you won't be surprised that we're doing a joint speech, seeing as how Zac can't do anything without me there to support him. And I mean *anything*.

ZAC: That's not strictly true, I once put the duvet cover on by myself.

HOLLY: You put one pillowcase on. And you made me do another one at the same time.

ZAC: I just like us to do things together, now that we're finally a couple. And an actual married one at that!

HOLLY: Yes, as most of you know, Zac and I knew each other at school.

ZAC: And if by 'knew each other' you mean we were in maths class together for a year and never spoke to each other then, yeah, I guess we did.

HOLLY: Ah wait, you did speak to me once. You asked me if you could have the answers because you had no idea what you were doing. But I didn't hand them over.

ZAC: I failed that test and got moved down a set so that ended any hopes of a maths romance.

HOLLY: You never were any good with numbers, were you?

ZAC: I wasn't any good with words either, judging by how successful I was at chatting you up.

HOLLY: I did actually fancy you at one point, but my friends told me not to bother. We were all about Edward Cullen from *Twilight* at the time: a mysterious, ghostly pale vampire with superhuman strength. Whereas you were more of a loud, tanned rugby boy who got sent out of a Geography lesson for throwing a protractor that accidentally hit the teacher in the head.

ZAC: That was a genuine accident! Anyway, enough about school, because our interactions there were minimal, and I needed time to grow into my body and change my entire personality before I had a chance with you. Which just so happened to be 16 years later.

HOLLY: We hadn't seen each other since school, then out of the blue, a Facebook message from the Z-Man himself. What were the odds of us getting together all those years later?

ZAC:	Don't ask me, I'm bad at maths remember.
HOLLY:	We got chatting and found out all about each other's lives. Zac hadn't long been single, so I was wary of him being on the rebound. We ended up just chatting for about a month before we even met.
ZAC:	We spoke every day. I'd look forward to her getting home from work so we could carry on with our conversation. I was 34 but I felt like a teenager again.
HOLLY:	Well you didn't throw a protractor at my head so that's something.
ZAC:	After a few weeks we decided to meet for a drink. When I was getting ready for our date, I was thinking a few months might've been better to give me a chance to take a few inches off my waistline. But I just had to wear black and hope for the best.
HOLLY:	We met and instantly hit it off. I could tell you were trying to impress me because you ordered a fancy wine. Then acted like you were a sommelier, swilling it round your mouth. I was getting hints of fruit, oak and . . . total bullshit.
ZAC:	Look, I knew you were way out of my league so I was trying to do everything I could to trick you into liking me.

HOLLY:	After that first meeting we began seeing each other more regularly, and eventually I decided it was time to introduce you to Maci.
HOLLY:	That was a big deal for me, because I knew it wasn't a decision you'd made lightly. And I was so nervous to meet her. What if she didn't like me? What if she felt uncomfortable? What if she could tell I knew nothing about wine?
HOLLY:	But she thought you were great. It helped that you brought her a magazine. More so because generally twelve-year-olds don't know what a magazine is. TikTok is their equivalent.
ZAC:	She did look a little bit confused by the magazine but it didn't take her long to accept me. And now I know all about TikTok. I've been roped into more dance challenges than I can remember. Surprisingly I haven't gone viral yet.
HOLLY:	You did go sort of viral once. We both did when we sent our proposal video to all of our friends, family and work group chats.
ZAC:	I think the kids would say it was 'poppin' off' – is that right Maci?

(Turn to Maci and wait for her reaction)

ZAC:	Yep, that's Maci never speaking to me again.

HOLLY:	Maci was actually part of the proposal. Some men ask their partner's father for their approval before they propose. But Zac asked Maci.
ZAC:	To me it was important to ask Maci first because she'd have to put up with me too. I said to her, if she thinks it's a good idea, she can help me make the proposal special for her mum. Thankfully, she thought it was a wonderful idea. An hour later she'd concocted a plan.
HOLLY:	I had no idea they'd been plotting. And one day I came home from work to be greeted by the pair of them in matching dog onesies, with paper flowers scattered everywhere. They told Alexa to play Taylor Swift and proceeded to do their synchronised dance.
ZAC:	I got down on one knee – partly because I needed a breather after the dance – and I took the ring out my sock.
HOLLY:	I said yes, of course. And finally conceded, the mess they'd made of the living room was worth it. Cut to a year later and here we are. It's been a bit of a whirlwind. Four years ago, we hadn't seen each other since we were wearing blazers and school bags. And now we're officially married. To the lad I once fancied from maths class.

ZAC:	And I couldn't be happier. I still can't believe I convinced you to marry me. I'll be forever grateful for us falling back into each other's lives.
HOLLY:	Okay before we get too soppy, we just want to say a few thank-yous. Firstly, to my mum and dad. You've always been there for me and have given me everything any daughter could hope for. You even forgave me for setting fire to the curtains when I was eighteen.
ZAC:	Yes, thank you Kate and Brian. I've loved getting to know you both over the last few years and I feel like I'm already part of your family. The bad news is, you're not ever getting rid of me now! Mum, I'd also like to thank you for everything. You've been by my side through thick and thin, and supported me through some rough times with both patience and humour. I know you are as delighted as me that Holly is now, officially, your daughter-in-law. And you look cracking today by the way.
HOLLY:	Yes, thank you Sheryl. You've been amazing with me from the start and you were a great support when we were moving in together. I'll never forget how welcome you made both me and Maci feel. Thank you for all that you've done for us both.

ZAC:	And finally, thank you to all of you for being with us here today. We're so lucky to have so many special people in our lives.
HOLLY:	Please join us as we propose a toast to a marriage made in maths class. I've no doubt, it adds up to something special.
HOLLY & ZAC:	To something special.

WRITTEN BY JAMES BOUGHEN

Bride speech – Delivered by Mikayla
Background: Mikayla has married Christian. They're based just outside Chicago, love travelling, and met in Australia. Christian's father, Dom, has recently passed away.

(*Light the candle on the top table*)

I promised Dom when he passed away that I'd make sure we remembered him at the wedding. In true Dom fashion, he said that dying was his sure-fire way of getting out of doing a toast, so I said that I'd stand up today and speak, so you can consider this a part-bride, part-father-of-the-groom speech. A mess, basically!

I thought it would be nice to have this candle on the top table to remember that a flame is the closest thing we have to actually seeing love. Like love, a flame can keep us warm.

The light from a flame can banish the darkness. It brings us all these amazing things, but it can still hurt us when we get too close.

Dom, wherever you are, please will you make a special note of the fact that it took me *forever* to find a candle in the Chicago Bulls colours, so you'd better appreciate it!

What I most wanted to say today is how lucky I am that I have found my light. Before I met him in the grubbiest, smelliest backpackers' hostel in Australia, perhaps the world, I had been fortunate to experience light in my life. My family and friends have shone brightly for me since I've known them and I want to thank them today for being here to celebrate with us.

But it was only when I met Christian that I understood how bright the light can become. And this light is just for me. And my light is just for him. I know others notice the light between us, but it's only my life that is warmed and brightened by it. I think that's wonderful.

Of course, I'd be letting him get away with too much if I claimed that Christian was exclusively a source of light! I'm hoping that James's best man speech will give us more information, but I will tell you that I first knew Christian as a source of a smell. Specifically, the smell of the worst hiking boots that have ever existed.

These boots were attached to Christian's feet for several weeks as he walked around Australia. Over the time that he'd been pretending to be waltzing Matilda, these boots had festered into fungal fun-houses. I'd been working at the hostel in Adelaide and when Christian booked a room, it was left to me to speak to this weird, bearded stick man about the smell emanating from his feet.

In typical Christian fashion, he apologised and immediately threw the boots in the bin behind the hostel. He then proceeded to go barefoot in Adelaide. Clearly, this was someone I needed to get to know more.

Since that time, Christian and I have travelled together on four of the seven continents. We've seen rainbows over Mount Fuji. We survived being mugged in Phuket by the drunkest mugger that has ever been. We also spent an entire week with what we think might have been dysentery in an Israeli kibbutz. Relationship experts should note that if you really, really want to know if your relationship will survive then you should try fighting for the ownership of a single toilet as one of you projectile vomits and the other tries to control explosive diarrhoea. In the end we found it easier to just buy a pack of corks.

Throughout it all we have laughed, we have learned about each other, and we started to love each other.

Life has been more serious since we returned home and found that Dom, Christian's beloved dad, had fallen very ill. We moved into the house with him and spent the next few months looking after him as best we could.

I've known that I loved Christian since he threw those boots in the bin, but it was during this time that I knew why. Just like Dom, Christian is someone who doesn't believe in getting caught up in the emotions of a situation, he prefers to focus on what he can do and as a result he has a gift for bypassing embarrassment.

It's really an amazing attribute, it meant that he was a perfect carer for Dom. I think it's also what makes him an incredible social worker. He doesn't have a judgmental bone in his body, he can talk to kings or tramps and treat them with the same love and dignity. I truly love and admire that about him.

About a month before he died Dom made us open all the booze in the house that he'd been saving for a rainy day. He realised it was a rainy day. For about two days we were as drunk as we've ever been. We drank £400 bottles of champagne and a 30-year-old whisky. Fortunately, the training that we'd had in that Israeli kibbutz came in handy.

During that time, Dom made us promise that we'd make sure that today was a huge party and that there wouldn't be any moping around. Dom wouldn't want you to waste any emotion on sadness, he'd rather you use that energy to make sure you got on the dance floor. That's why we're having a ceilidh tonight, because there's no chance of sitting out the dancing. If you're not normally a dancer, consider it your wedding gift to us.

As we start our married life together, we don't feel like it's overshadowed by Dom's death. We feel like it's warmed by the light of his love. So, as I finish my speech, I'd like to propose a toast to the man I love and to love itself.

You'll see on the table there are loads of candles and lighters. I'd love it if you could take a candle and light one, or two, or even more, for people you love. It doesn't have to be someone who is no longer here, it could be someone in this room. It could be someone who knows about that love and who reciprocates it. Or it could be for someone who is oblivious to your love.

That's it, just place your candle on the table and the venue have kindly said they'll switch the lights off for my toast. Thank you. Wow!

Now as you look around, you can see just how much love there is. You might even be able to feel the warmth of it.

You can see how kindly it lights the faces of everyone who sees it and how people smile when they see it.

Could you raise your glasses with me and drink to Dom, to Christian and to love.

To love.

WRITTEN BY ANDREW SHANAHA

Gay groom speech – Delivered by Sam
Background: Sam has married Miles. They met at work and live in Leeds, England.

Friends, family, plus-ones we had to invite out of awkwardness, it's a pleasure to have you all here.

In my job, I tend to write down my ideas, tweet them or pop them in a press release, rather than say them out loud to the 120 people I love the most in the whole wide world. However, even I know that tweeting this speech wouldn't quite have the same emotional pull. And unfortunately for you lot, this speech definitely wouldn't fit the 280-character limit.

For those of you who don't know me, I'm Sam, and you must have walked into the wrong wedding.

Now, I, Sam, recently came to the conclusion that I am the luckiest man in the history of humankind. That's right: I firmly and truly believe that nobody has ever been as lucky as Sam O'Riley.

Not Joan R. Ginther, the Texan woman who won the lottery a staggering four times in the 1990s. Not twelfth-century Japanese monk 'Nichiren', who survived his own beheading when his executioner was struck by lightning. Not even Lucky Luckersson, the Swedish horseshoe maker and four-leafed clover collector I just made up.

Because none of those people were lucky enough to marry Miles Wilson.

And yes, some of you may be thinking, 'Surely it's not all luck – you probably won him over with your winning personality, your effortless charm and your wicked sense of humour.' And to those people I say, 'Look, I already told you, you're at the wrong wedding.'

My first piece of luck came on the day my firm were hired as clients by Miles's company, and I found out who I'd be dealing with on the accounts side. Then Smelly Frank died of a heart attack and Miles took his place.

The first time I saw him, I genuinely knew Miles was the man I wanted to spend the rest of my life with. And not just because Smelly Frank's passing had made me worry about how much time I had left.

To clarify, by the way, Smelly Frank never existed. I'm pretty sure you're allowed to speak ill of the dead if you invented them for comic effect.

When I first met Miles, the first thing I noticed were his huge, green eyes and his effortless, innocent smile that said, 'I'm not the kind of man who invents smelly men then kills them off for a cheap laugh.' He was just so darn attractive, and I couldn't believe my luck when he matched that aesthetic beauty with a witty, playful personality and a kind, generous, empathetic soul.

Honestly, the only way Miles could have been more perfect was if he was the manager of Tottenham Hotspur and wanted to pick me up front. Although for anyone who's ever seen me play five-a-side, there's an argument that my limited ability would put something of a strain on our relationship.

Of course, me being me, I was way too nervous to ask him out, umming and ahhing my way through awkward conversations and pretending to care about work during our meetings, when all I could think about was him. My hesitation and nerves lasted so long that I almost missed my chance, but thankfully fate was about to strike again.

This next lucky break came when I was staying in London on an overnight with work, and my colleague and close friend Sachin had a family emergency and had to cancel his trip. Although now I think about it, I guess that's more lucky for me than for Sachin . . . Sorry mate, hope your auntie's okay now.

I emailed Miles and told him the news, that it would just be me in town for the evening, and that I'd be having dinner on my own in the hotel, and he immediately suggested I come out with him and an old school friend instead. Delighted, I said yes, and then I was even more delighted to learn that this school friend wouldn't be joining us. Because he never existed in the first place. Yes, my husband likes to make up people too.

We had an incredible night, laughing, talking, eating and drinking so much that our meetings the next day were mostly made up of orange Lucozade, Big Mac meals and enough Paracetamol to knock out a large buffalo.

After a few weeks, the work arrangement came to an end, but mine and Miles's relationship didn't. I'd spend weekends in London, then he'd spend weekends in Bath, and we'd talk on the phone most evenings. I think O2's profits got a significant boost that summer.

And the good fortune didn't even stop there. I was lucky enough that he agreed to switch offices to Bath so he could move in with me. I was lucky enough to meet his amazing, hilarious friends and kind, welcoming family. I was lucky enough that we found Pogo the Yorkshire Terrier at the shelter, who quickly became the most adored third wheel you could hope to meet.

Finally, I was lucky enough that, when I again ummed and ahhed about how to ask him to marry me, Miles cottoned on, and asked me instead. And he was *unlucky* enough that I immediately said yes.

Miles, I love you, and today the luckiest man in the world has also become the happiest.

Before I go, thanks must go to my mum and dad, Jill and Colin, for blessing me with all this good luck in the first place, as well as doing your best to pass down your kindness, your ambition, your sense of fun and your unending loyalty. If Miles and I can be even a fraction of the absolute power couple you two are, it will be a job well done.

To Miles's parents, Jim and Ursula, thanks for all your help and support in the lead-up to this big day, for welcoming me like a son, and of course for raising this total force of nature I'm so proud to call my husband.

And finally, I wanted to thank whatever it is that brings us luck. Whether it's fate, a god, multiple gods, the universe itself or simply chance, luck is what brought us here today. Which is why, under your napkins, each of you will find a small gift from me. A lottery ticket for tonight.

And if any of you win, I *assume* I'll be lucky enough that you'll wire me half. I have a free bar to pay for tonight, after all.

That's all from me, but before I go, please join me by raising your glasses in a toast to the biggest jackpot of them all – to Miles!

WRITTEN BY ED AMSDEN AND TOM COLES

Stage 2 – Gather Your Speech Content

Okay. This is the fun part.

This is where you get to reminisce about your relationship, and the chapter where you discover you're actually a creative genius.

This is also the stage where I encourage you to have lots of date nights, order in some takeaways and mute your notifications. Devote some time to this stage and the following ones will be so much easier.

The plan

In this chapter, we'll cover ...

- The **building blocks** you need to write a great speech.
- **Where and when to start.**
- **Modern etiquette** – your thank-yous and toasts to absent friends and family.
- How to **hunt down your best anecdotes.**
- How to **be funny without resorting to googled gags.**
- How to **be romantic without using clichés or platitudes.**
- How to **source and use quotes.**

EXPERT INSIGHT

'I think the aim of every wedding speech should be to unite the room and create a sense of inclusiveness. The story you're telling should appeal to everyone and make them feel connected, engaged and ideally it will also evoke emotion.

'I always encourage my clients to throw the rules out. Every aspect of the wedding (including the speeches) should feel unique to the couple and not formulaic.'

COLLEEN KENNEDY COHEN

'For people who don't know where to start, I always like to quote one of my favourite authors, Ernest Hemingway: "Write the truest sentence you know".'

ZOE BURKE

'The newlyweds' speech should be insight into the home-life of the couple. It should reveal the secret little stories and give a snapshot into their relationship.'

ED AMSDEN AND TOM COLES

'Think about the genuine moments that have made you smile and try to be yourself. Hopefully, if they're marrying you, your partner might quite like that!'

KAT WILLIAMS

'A wedding speech is a permanent, public expression of your love. Unlike the cake, it's a memory that will last decades. It's one of the biggest gifts you will ever give your partner.'

ANDREW SHANAHAN

'For me, a great wedding speech is one that gets everyone to pause the party for a second and remember the fantastic love story they're there to celebrate. At the end of the day, a wedding is about two people choosing one another and starting a life together. The best speeches bring everyone together, no matter whose half of the guestlist they were on!'

HAMISH SHEPHARD

'The ceremony was about you. The speech is about your guests. Let them know that you're honoured for them to be there, thank them from the heart and get them in the mood to party with you on this amazing day.'

ALAN BERG

'I studied maths at uni and believe maths rules the world, even when it comes to storytelling. Life, love, speeches – nothing follows a linear line.

'A great speech needs peaks and troughs. It needs happiness and sadness; light and shade. It needs to take people on a journey to add up to something special.'

SHAI HUSSAIN

'Often you only actually know one half of the couple really well, so the speeches give you a crucial insight into who your friend is marrying and their relationship.

'Then you can sit back and decide if you approve or not!'

CLAIRE WETTON

YOUR WEDDING SPEECH CHECKLIST

Before we start gathering content, let's look at what we want (and *don't* want).

This is based on a Speechy checklist that I created for our team of writers.

Ensure:

1 Humour within the first twenty seconds.
2 A welcome that feels more than a cut-and-paste job.
3 An insight into your relationship.
4 At least one great anecdote.

5 A tribute to your partner that's unique, honest and meaningful.
6 Thank-yous that are genuinely touching.
7 Regular touches of humour throughout.
8 An emotional sucker punch and/or a killer line.

As well as the 'to do' list, we inevitably have a 'please, don't' list . . .
    Avoid:

1 Clichés and platitudes.
2 Googled gags or wedding-speech jokes.
3 Edgy humour or OTT swearing.
4 A long list of thank-yous.
5 Handing out gifts.
6 A eulogy to the dearly departed.
7 Unnecessary wedding waffle.
8 Too many adjectives, not enough evidence of them.

Some points seem more nebulous than others but it's a great list to refer to *prior* to writing your speech, and something to check against *after* you've written your first draft.

YOUR PEP TALK

If that checklist sent you into a bit of a panic, don't worry. Even if the best thing you've ever written is a humorous message on WhatsApp, I'm going to guide you through this speech writing process step by step.

Talking about love, opening your heart and soul to your nearest and dearest, is not something we often do. The rise of social media may mean that the world is more 'connected', but we're spending more time alone, separated from our families, removed from a sense of community.

We're now more used to *typing* how we feel than telling our mates IRL. I mean, we live in an era where we have an acronym for 'in real life'.

Consequently, it's not surprising that speaking in public is a big deal. And increasingly so.

But here's the thing: no amount of virtual likes from your online 'friends' will ever replace the glow you get from looking round a room full of people you love and seeing them smile back at you. That's real emotion, unfiltered, not airbrushed. That's proper joy.

The truth is, *most* people think writing a wedding speech is the hardest, most soul-destroying thing they've had to do in a long time. But, I promise you, the effort is worth it.

Say hello to your co-writer

Whether you're giving a solo speech, a joint speech or each of you is giving a speech, it's better if you two work together.

I firmly believe creativity is infectious.

In the BBC Writersroom, no idea is a bad idea. Or even if it *is*, no one points it out.

Bad ideas are part of the process. Jerry Seinfield, Amy Schumer, Romesh Ranganathan, Peter Kay, Kevin Hart; I guarantee whoever makes you laugh has *a lot* of rubbish ideas. They just pick the best ones to share with other people.

If your partner comes up with a lame joke, resist the urge to roll your eyes, bang your head on the table and wail 'What's the point?' Instead, *play* with the idea; humour it, view it as a springboard to new ideas.

Getting started

Start soon. As soon as possible. Now. Before now. Just start.

Don't read this book, think you're sorted and come back to it a fortnight before the wedding. Start working on your speech at least a couple of *months* before. (Of course, if you're reading this a week before the big day, ignore all this 'start early' advice but, you know, *do* start.)

The bad news is writing takes effort. If you want your speech to be unique, you're going to need to do more than steal the best lines from our speech examples (though do help yourself to a few of them).

If in doubt, write *anything*. Bullet points. The chronological benchmarks of your relationship. An anecdote. An observation. Anything is better than nothing. It gives you something to improve.

And you'll find, as soon as you start *genuinely* thinking about your speech (not just that abstract 'I really should *start* thinking about my speech'), you'll find material starts popping into your head when you least expect it.

In fact, be warned, after reading this chapter, you may find yourself bombarded with ideas, even when you don't want them. Prepare yourself for them.

Prepare for ideas

- Use a note-sorting app.
- Create a folder on your phone for your voicenotes.
- Leave an old-school pad and paper by your bed.
- Flick through this book before going on any commute and fire up your brain to trawl your unconscious for creative, poignant and genius lines.
- Find your 'thinking spot'. Some writers go for a walk, some have a coffee break, I have a shower. Weird, I know, but if I'm really stuck on a speech I have a shower and, nine times out of ten, it solves my problem. One day I ended up having three showers. I had two cracking speeches by the end of the day, and, hell, was I clean!

As Andrew Shanahan says, 'If you start working on your speech a long time before the wedding, you're basically guaranteed to deliver a good speech. It really is as simple as that.'

Stop hitting the snooze button and engage your mind.

THE WEDDING SPEECH BUILDING BLOCKS

There's no point trying to write your speech before you know what's going in it. It's like baking; you need to source the best possible ingredients to make a cake that's so darn good you resent sharing it with other people (or is that just me?).

We have to get our building blocks in place before we can craft something wonderful, and when it comes to your speech, our first job is to hunt down the best possible content.

When the Speechy team first started working with clients, we'd chat to them on the phone and interview them prior to starting their speech. It was surprising how difficult a lot of people found articulating what they loved about their partner. The clients' responses were generally pretty generic and, dare I say it, boring.

Of course, it was *our* fault.

Every couple has an exciting story to tell. We just needed to ask better questions.

It took us a while to figure out which questions elicited the best responses, and then a bit longer to realise that not everyone could be immediately insightful.

We designed a questionnaire, with cracking questions, that people could answer in their own time (sometimes over a few hours, sometimes over a couple of weeks). This helped clients get their brains into gear and come up with better quality building blocks for us to work with.

In this chapter, I'll share the questions we now ask our clients and the techniques we use to gather the best possible speech material.

As our writer Andrew Shanahan advises, 'Don't ask yourself the big questions first. Don't immediately try to describe the depth of love you feel for someone. Your brain will freeze.

'Instead, you need to scratch away at the subject matter and slowly reveal the warmth that's there.'

BUILDING BLOCK 1 – THE ETIQUETTE

Okay, let's get the etiquette out of the way as it's something speakers panic about and it's easy to get sucked down a rabbit hole.

Let's start by saying (again) there are no wedding speech rules. When it comes to etiquette, it's simply a case of common sense and being polite. Honestly, that's it.

With a newlywed speech it's just about:

- Welcoming your guests.
- Paying a tribute to your partner (sounds odd but some speakers have been known to forget this).
- Thanking the main wedding party – family and close friends who have helped in the run-up and on the day.
- A tribute to the dearly departed if necessary.
- A heart-warming toast.

Despite what some guides suggest, you do not need to . . .

- Address everyone as 'ladies and gentlemen'.
- Hand out gifts.
- Namecheck everyone who has worked behind the scenes.
- Thank the venue, caterers or anyone you've paid.
- Thank people who have travelled far.
- Conclude by toasting the bridesmaids (in fact, I think it's odd if you do these days).

Andrew Shanahan agrees: 'It's important that you know what modern wedding speech etiquette is just so you can decide if it's relevant to you. It's not rules you have to follow, just codified reminders.

'I never slavishly follow etiquette guides but I use them as a tick box cheat sheet. Most of it is just sensible suggestions.'

The thank-yous – Who to thank

The thank-yous are obviously very important but you also need to be wary of turning your speech into one long tedious list.

Think about those Oscar winners who thank a list of folk you've never heard of. It's dull.

For guests, thank-yous are really only interesting if 1) they're personally getting thanked or 2) the thank-yous are entertaining, from the heart and feel more than a cut-and-paste job.

Do not waste your word count thanking some random cousin for travelling hundreds of miles to be with you. Thank them personally, yes, but they don't need an individual namecheck in the speech.

Of course, it's important that the thank-yous are fair and tactful. Even if you're not a huge fan, it might still be worth mentioning your dad's new partner. And if you're thanking your friend for her help with the wedding invites, make sure you thank your aunt for her contributions to the day's décor.

Once you get into thanking people who aren't part of the 'top table', it can be hard to know when to stop. If it starts to feel overwhelming or monotonous, see if you can group your thank-yous, for example, 'the uni girls' or 'the Campbell clan'.

Personally, I'd never want to skimp on the thank-yous to the parents (and if you've both got time on the mic, make sure you thank your parents *and* your new in-laws).

However, if you're wanting to keep the thank-yous minimal (and give more personal thanks in person earlier or later in the day), then you *can* group all parents together (sometimes this is actually the most diplomatic option if there are remarriages and step-partners involved too).

For example, your thank-yous may be directed at the following groups of people ...

- Parents (and their partners).
- Wider family (if necessary).

- Close friends who have helped with the wedding prep and survived the stag and hen dos.
- Children (either your step or shared children).
- Everyone for coming.

Even in a brutal form, you need to summarise each group within a couple of sentences.

For example 'Thank you to our parents – old and new – all of whom have added something wonderful to our lives. Thank you for contributing to the people we are today. And only you can decide if that's a compliment or not.'

The thank-yous – How to thank

GIFTS

Firstly, do *not* give gifts! Certainly not as part of the speech at least.

Whenever couples try to hand out bouquets or any gift during their speeches, it results in an awkward moment. The speaker has to pause mid-flow, there's a lot of palaver getting the gift to the recipient, and inevitably, an uncomfortable silence. You end up wishing there was a heckler in the audience!

So, avoid the gift-giving. It's a bit 'showy' anyway. Deliver the gift in a heartfelt and more intimate way earlier or later in the day.

WORDS

When it comes to your thank-yous, step away from the clichés. You don't want to seem like you're simply ticking off the etiquette 'to dos', you want the person you're thanking to feel truly cherished.

Your thanks shouldn't just relate to the wedding prep. It should be about what these people have brought to your life. And don't worry, this doesn't need to be overly pious. Ideally, the thank-yous should contain humour too.

We'll cover how to pay a tribute to your partner later in the book (page 88) but the same principles apply. Avoid platitudes. Stay clear of adjectives. Pinpoint their unique character and the individual nature of your relationship.

THANK-YOU INSPIRATION

Your parents	'Thank you to my parents. I've been spoilt with a lifetime of love – unfaltering even through my thrash metal phase.
	'Thank you for knowing me better than I've known myself and for all the guidance that you've given me over the years. It's not always been welcomed but it's always been right. You always knew being a hip-hop artist wasn't for me.
	'Your support over the years has been priceless, though when you consider the free rent and the amount of dad's secret cider stash I've drunk as a teenager, it's probably more in the region of £180k.
	'Please do help yourself to an extra slice of cake!'
Your mother-in-law	'I'd like to thank my new mum-in-law for welcoming me into the (Surname) family and introducing me to all its wonderful traditions. Who knew you could have key lime pie for breakfast?
	'I also have to thank her for passing down such amazing traits to my new partner. These two share the same infectious laugh, determined spirit and, unfortunately, unwavering support for Manchester United.

	'Julie – if I didn't already have a fantastic mother, I think I'd want to be adopted by you. Though, considering who I've just married, that might be a bit weird.'
Friends	'Thanks to Jim and the rest of the motley crew who make up my ushers.
	'These boys have supported me through the good times, they've supported me through the bad times, and every Friday, they've supported me home from the pub.
	'Seriously, these are the mates who I can call on at 4am and I know that they'll answer. These are the mates who will listen to yet another of my ludicrous business ideas without laughing. And these are the mates who I know will last me a lifetime.
	'Thanks fellas.'
Stepchild	'I'm so chuffed that marrying (your partner) means I also have (*your step-son*) in my life.
	'I realise it's a big disappointment to him that I have no idea who Master Wu is but at least we share a mutual appreciation of chicken nuggets. And I must say I'm also gutted they're not on the menu today.
	'Seriously, this little man has taught me so much over the years, most importantly, how to love and look after his mum.
	'He really is one of life's unexpected joys.'

EXTRA THANKS

If you find you have too much to say to anyone, write them a letter to open on the morning of the wedding.

We encourage a lot of the fathers we work with to do this if their word count is reaching its limit and they're frustrated by how much they still have to say.

A letter is actually a lovely idea as it provides an extra sense of connection between you and your loved ones within the context of a very busy day.

Thank-you notes are also great for the some of the special people you're not namechecking in the speech. This is different to the standard 'thank you for the gift' note that gets sent weeks later. This is a letter that they should ideally have on the morning of the wedding that acknowledges how meaningful they are to you.

Anna Price Olson says, 'We're actually seeing quite a few couples writing personal notes to all their guests to read at the reception dinner. It's a lovely thing for people to sit down and be reminded of their personal connection with the newlyweds.'

TOASTS

You don't need to toast everyone you thank. In fact, the only toasts I'd encourage you to propose are one at the end of your speech and one (if it's necessary) to the dearly departed.

If you propose a toast to everyone on your thank-you list, then it becomes tedious, especially with the guests having to stand up and sit down again in quick succession.

Your turn

Now it's your chance to get creative with your thank-yous.
Simply write a list of all the people you want to thank. Then
work out which of them you want to thank *within* the speech
itself (i.e. the top tier thank-yous!).

Next, brainstorm why exactly you want to thank them. Try to
add both heartfelt sentiment and humour to each of them if
you can.

A thank-you should be between 50 and 100 words.

The dearly departed

How you handle the loss of a loved one very much depends on how
raw the emotions are. And, even if you think you 'have things under
control', a wedding can heighten or even reignite a sense of grief.
Prepare for that.

At the same time, don't turn your speech into a eulogy. A
wedding speech needs to be joyful, so think about thoughtful and
upbeat ways you can acknowledge an absent loved one. Don't put
yourself in the position of giving a speech where you get overly
emotional and have to stop.

There *are* ways to paying tribute to a loved one whilst still
ensuring your speech is a celebration. The key is to think of ways
to remember them with a smile.

Here are some ideas to consider.

1 – PAY A TRIBUTE TO YOUR LOVED ONES BEFORE
THE WEDDING

Give your raw emotion an outlet before the day itself.

If the person in question is a close relative or has died recently,
pay a more substantial tribute to them in the week leading up to

the wedding. This could be over a dinner with friends and family or it could just be a more casual visit to a place that meant something to you both.

This is a time to reflect on your favourite memories of them as well as imagine what they would have loved about your wedding day. Here, tears can flow, meaning on the day, your loved one's absence won't feel quite so alien.

2 – BE CREATIVE
On the actual day, think of nice touches that guests will associate with the person you love. For example . . .

- Could your favours be pots of homemade jam made using your beloved gran's secret recipe?
- Could your guests join you in a toast to your father by drinking his favourite malt?
- Could the tables be decorated with forget-me-nots in honour of your friend?

Rather than sombre or sad, be creative and considerate.

3 – THOUGHTFUL FAVOURS
More charities are giving couples the chance to donate to them by purchasing wedding favours. Guests are presented with a simple card on their table, showing your support for the cause.
It's a great way to remember a loved one in a truly meaningful way.

4 – CANDLES
You will see in the speech example on page 46 how powerful candles can be in honouring absent loved ones.

5 – SCHEDULE THE TEARS FOR LATER IN THE SPEECH
Lots of speakers make the mistake of mentioning absent friends

and family too early in the speech, making it hard to change gear and move on to the more celebratory and humorous content.

By positioning your tribute towards the end of your speech, you also ensure you don't get choked up too soon.

If you feel that you *are* about to cry, try looking upwards. It is said to be physically impossible to cry if you are looking up. Of course, everyone will understand if you do.

Dearly departed inspiration

'Of course there's someone who's missing today and that's my dad. He never got to meet Sophie but I know he would have loved her.

'I can only hope I've learnt from the best when it comes to being a good husband.

'Dad taught me that marrying a woman you love is an honour not to be taken lightly. He showed me the value of honesty, patience and respecting your partner's point of view, even when it's wildly different to your own.

'Most of all, he taught me how important it is to laugh and, with Sophie by my side, that's something I hope to do every day for the rest of my life.

'So here's to my wonderful father ... To Martin.'

BUILDING BLOCK 2 – STORY HUNTING

It might seem obvious that your wedding speech needs a good story in it but a lot of wedding speeches *don't*.

They should.

Why stories matter

Neuroscientists have discovered that our brains light up when we hear stories. It seems humans are programmed to be empathic; we're literally designed to be curious about other people.

One of our prime instincts in life is to love and so we're all naturally, intrinsically fascinated by love stories. Which means you're on to a winner here.

Telling a good story helps sync your mind with your guests. When people hear an engaging story, they put themselves in your shoes and that process forms a deeper connection. Just like that.

Finding cracking anecdotes (short stories) is a crucial part of creating a great speech. And, to reassure you, we *all* have brilliant stories, even the desperate grooms I speak to who are convinced they're 'just a boring couple who don't do anything exciting'.

A story doesn't need to be long. It doesn't need to be extraordinary. It just has to reveal something about you as a couple.

The good news is, we're all born storytellers. And this chapter will make you even better.

Expert insight

> *'When guests hear great stories, they feel less of a spectator at the wedding and more like they're involved. As an Asian man, I go to loads of weddings and if you're one of 500 guests, you might not know the couple very well. A good speech helps me connect with them.'*
>
> SHAI HUSSAIN

> *'Ultimately all you need is three good stories. Actually even one really great one can make a speech fantastic.'*
>
> KAT WILLIAMS

> *'When we start writing a speech, the first thing we both do is hunt out the best stories. Three or four ideally. We'll literally just bash them out and whack them down on the blank page. Everything goes from there.'*
>
> ED AMSDEN AND TOM COLES

Story don'ts

Don't bother with . . .

- **The proposal story** – This is only interesting if it went wrong in some way. Detailing the romantic way you, or your partner, popped the question is generally predictable (it's *meant* to be romantic) or seen as an attempt to show off.
- **The stag / hen / bachelor party / bridal shower** – Sure, thank your teams for organizing them and feel free to allude to any bad behaviour but do not consider this an 'anecdote'. Again, these events often involve drinking too much and someone embarrassing themselves.
- **Long or complicated stories** – Generally (and there are exceptions), you need to be able to tell the story within about 100 words.

Story dos

Look for stories that ...

- Tell the audience something **new** about you, your partner or love (or at least offer a fresh look at one of your classic tales).
- Provide **insight** into your relationship.
- Are **funny** *or* **poignant** and **thought-provoking.**
- **Are easy to follow.**
- **Have a point**. A good story needs a clear, central message that fits with the theme of the rest of the speech (we'll get to that!).

Story hunt hackathon

If you start your story-hunt by asking 'What are our best, funniest, most insightful stories?' chances are you won't come up with much, so here are a few tried and tested ways to kick-start your search.

A good story doesn't need to be a major event or particularly important. A good storyteller can create drama, tension and comedy from the more mundane acts; like the tension of asking someone to go on a date.

Don't worry about the stories being fully formed, having a meaningful message or a killer punchline at this stage. But, start to notice if there is a running theme that connects any of the anecdotes.

Now, let's see what stories you can come up with ...

1 – SEMINAL STORIES

The cornerstones of any relationship are likely to be interesting.

Even if you suspect that the majority of your guests know where you met, your retelling of the story may provide some refreshing insight.

Here's a list of the classic 'love stories' to consider ...

- How you met.
- The first date.
- Meeting the parents.
- Going on your first holiday together.
- Moving in together.
- When you discovered they weren't actually perfect.
- Any embarrassing anecdotes.
- Any challenges you've overcome together (comedic or otherwise).
- Any classic stories that you've enjoyed telling friends and that still make you laugh.

2 – STORIES THAT CAN BE USED IN EVIDENCE

The opening moment of a film is often an establishing scene where we learn about the central character. It usually runs for just a few minutes and concentrates on the mundane reality of that person's existence before the plot kicks in.

These crucial seconds are designed to tell us everything we need to know about that character and it's the small things that often give it away.

Are they scoffing down their breakfast in the car whilst swearing at a red light, or are they eating their porridge whilst listening to Radio 4 and reading *Time* magazine? Often, a ten-second scene tells us more than a two-page biography would.

Little things can reveal a lot and that's the sort of stories we're hunting for here. The ones that stop you using lazy adjectives!

Adjectives are white noise in a speech and they're a lazy tool in the writer's arsenal. They're overused and easy to forget. It's also easy to assume they're not even true.

Unless, of course, you *prove* they are.

Bring the adjectives to life with real-life examples. Show these adjectives in action.

So, here's your next writing task. Think of three character

traits that could be considered questionable in your partner. Not bad exactly, but not something they'd put on their CV.

Now, under each heading think of three anecdotes or circumstances where they have shown that quality in action.

Here's an example of how it might look.

(If your partner is ...) Greedy	(If your partner is ...) Forgetful	(If your partner is ...) Loud
We once had an hour-long argument after I stole a spoonful of their risotto. We now refer to it as risotto-gate.	Forgot where they parked the car and phoned the police to report it missing.	Neighbours (a household of students) had to complain to *us* – after we watched a football match on TV and they got overly excited.
On our first date, they ordered a steak. I was too nervous to eat so they ate my chicken Milanese too. We also shared a dessert. I had about two spoonfuls.	They spent the majority of a year thinking that they were a year older than they were. They found out after they started planning their 30th and their friends informed them the party was slightly premature.	They've been asked to laugh quieter at two separate restaurants.
When we told them we were moving, the staff at Pizza Express cried.	When helping with our six-year-old's homework, they forgot how many days were in a year. They taught them it was 356 and that's still ingrained in daughter, even now in high school.	

Okay, so sometimes there isn't that third killer example but you get the idea.

This exercise prompts you to work hard on coming up with good content. And, hopefully, stops you resorting to lazy adjectives.

3 – STORY TRIGGERS

Sometimes you need a few prompts to get that brain working, like their online profile that claimed a passion for history but didn't quite reveal this 'interest' would involve you having to visit military museums in every town and country you go to with them.

See if you can hunt down . . .

- Your online dating profiles (if you met there).
- If you met at work, do you still have your contract or job description? It could be used for comedy purposes.
- If you're childhood sweethearts, hunt out the school reports.
- And, obviously, look back at your photos through the years. This will inevitably trigger memories but *don't* consider using them as part of your speech.*

---

*The dreaded PowerPoint speech

The days of PowerPoint speeches with photo montages are OVER.

Photos of the newlyweds with bad hair or embarrassing themselves are no longer funny. Photos of them looking cute, even as a child, don't add much either.

This rule applies to best mates and parent speeches too. Warn them, there is no PowerPoint available on site.

Just no.

BUILDING BLOCK 3 – FINDING YOUR FUNNY

The priority placed on humour varies with clients around the world.

Generally, folk from the UK and Australia want their speeches to have a lot of humour in them, while clients from other parts of the world, namely the US, lean towards a sweeter speech, with lighter elements, as opposed to all-out funny.

Some of the influencers I spoke to said that there shouldn't be any pressure on the speaker to be funny. 'If you're not naturally funny, don't try to be,' seemed to be a prevalent view. You might be of a similar view: 'I'm not funny, so let's not try to be.'

But, and I'm sorry if you were hoping for a get-out clause there, I disagree.

Yes, I admit, speakers should 'work with what they got' but I also believe people can improve and supercharge what they've got.

While no wedding speaker should be trying to deliver a stand-up routine, all speakers *should* aim to make their audience *smile*. And not a polite smile, but a hearty involuntary one.

Humour is *not* the reserve of 'funny people'. Neither should it be assumed that being funny is hard.

Yes, there are some folk who are just naturally funny but I'm not sure if all the comedy writers who work on Speechy could be described as 'funny people'. We certainly *write* comedy material but are we natural extroverts known for making our mates laugh? Are we 'the funny one'? Well, no, actually.

I'm as slow as the next person when it comes to witty comebacks but I've managed to become a comedy writer because I recognise it's a skill and it's something I've worked at.

In this chapter, I'll share some of the techniques I've found most helpful over the years.

Firstly though ...

Why humour matters

Learning to be funny (or at least, funnier) is a useful life skill.

- Humour lowers defences and **makes your audience like you more** (honestly, scientists far cleverer than me have proved it).
- Humour has the same effect as learning something new does on the brain. It **wakes up an audience and helps them remember the content of your speech.**
- Humour is a well-established **ingratiation tactic**. Laughter is a scientifically recognised social bonding juice.

In her TED Talk, neuroscientist Sophie Finn said, 'Laughter is more like an animal call than speech.' It's a primitive but powerful social connection. And it's one you should be tapping into.

Laughter is not only good for your wedding speech, it's good for you and improves the delivery of your speech. It increases your energy and improves your breathing. It also releases lovely endorphins, otherwise known as the 'happy hormone'. And, if you get a laugh in the first twenty seconds of your speech, it will immediately relax you and your audience.

Laughter is infectious, so the first audible titter can result in a hearty group response. Humour can also help make your romantic and profound content so much more powerful. The sweet stuff shines more if you've already been disarmingly honest, funny, and self-depreciating.

The lesson here is, don't be shy about trying to find your funny bone. Making people laugh is not about 'being a funny person', it's simply about putting the effort in.

Expert insight

'The South Asian community is now recognising the importance of humour. The wedding speeches used to just be a chance for the father to show off about their children's achievements but luckily, speeches are getting better and edgier. Now, the younger generation are definitely having a laugh on the mic which is great to see.'

SHAI HUSSAIN

'Even with the funny stories, it has to have a point. Don't tell me about the drunken trip on holiday or whatever; tell me something that has a meaning to it, something that ties into the theme of the speech. Even the humour has to feel connected and revealing.'

EDUARDO BRANIFF

'What I don't like is when a wedding speech is taken too far and instead of recalling a funny moment, it brings up something embarrassing that shouldn't be shared. We have to know the limits when it comes to sharing, especially in front of a big crowd.'

ELEONORA TUCCI

'You might have a good anecdote, a fun night out that's legendary, but it might not actually have much of a punchline. Always hunt the punchline.'

ED AMSDEN AND TOM COLES

'Love goes without saying if you're getting married, but if you can lovingly tease your partner, it can add a sense of realism. For example, 'I love you even after you've been eating cheesy Wotsits.'

CLAIRE WETTON

Humour don'ts

Telling a bad joke is worse than no joke. Avoid . . .

- **Anything edgy** – Think Chris Rock at the Oscars. It's just not worth the risk. Some punchlines ain't worth the punch.
- **A tasteless joke** – Grooms thanking their in-laws for the gift of their daughter and adding that they'll enjoy 'unwrapping her later tonight'. Cringe. In a recent Guides for Brides poll, 74 per cent of people said they want their wedding speeches 'clean', and that's a young demographic.
- **Anything about exes** – While you and your partner might find it funny, your in-laws might not think it's appropriate.
- **A long lead-up to a punchline** – If it takes too long to get to the laugh, drop it. Jokes are funnier the punchier they are.
- **'In' jokes** – Do you really want people to feel like they're not part of the party?
- **Any of the old wedding gags** – 'Without all of you here today, it wouldn't have been the same . . . but it would have been cheaper.' 'Let me tell you that is not the first time today I have risen from a warm seat with a bit of paper in my hand.' And so on . . . Basically, if the joke could be used in someone else's wedding speech, it shouldn't be in yours.
- **Anything based on outdated assumptions or prejudices** – 'What's the difference between in-laws and out-laws? Outlaws are wanted.' 'I've got a very funny speech prepared for you, but my wife has told me to read this one instead.' Etc, etc.
- **Religious or cultural jokes** – Only ever appropriate if they're yours to make.
- **Politics or contentious issues** – You may take it for granted that the people you love feel the same way as you about 'the big stuff' but that's rarely the case. For example, an anti-vax joke *may* go down well with a portion of your audience but you can't assume everyone will appreciate it. Avoid playing to your own echo chamber.

Please note: having even *one* googled gag in your speech will take the shine off any of the original lines you've crafted. People will assume you've stolen them all so stay away from any generic wedding humour.

Humour dos

- **Keep it original.**
- **Have humour within the first three sentences.**
- **Have regular touches of humour throughout the speech.** You don't want more than 30 seconds without giving your guests the opportunity to smile.

Humour hackathon

So how the hell do you find this crucial humour?

Well, work through the following prompts and you're guaranteed to come up with the comedy goods.

1 – SURPRISE YOUR AUDIENCE

When the Speechy team work with clients, one of the questions we ask is, 'Tell us something about your partner that nobody else knows.'

'That question gets people to think differently,' say Ed Amsden and Tom Coles. 'It's not what people would naturally think about when they're sitting down to write a speech but it elicits great material.'

Sharing a little revelation with your guests wakes them up and makes your speech memorable.

Sometimes clients tell us something brilliant but then worry that it's *too* revealing.

But actually when we dig down that's not always the case. Sometimes it just needs to be written in a way that takes the sting out of it.

So have a think ... **Is there anything about your partner or your relationship that people don't know?**

It could be ...

PROMPT	INSPIRATION
A party trick that only you know about	Their ass claps when they jump. They've now developed quite a repertoire of rhythmic beats to amuse us when we're bored.
A weird claim to fame	They won a hula-hooping competition when they were a teenager. And they've kept the trophy.
An embarrassing secret	They don't know their times table and can't work out percentages unless it's 100% or 50%.
A relationship revelation	We split up (for 24 hours) over a debate about politics. We've subsequently agreed never to discuss Boris Johnson or Trump again.
A confession	It was *me* who accidently split red wine on my new in-laws' sofa, not their neighbours who I tried to blame it on at the time.

Obviously some revelations might not be suitable to share but check in with each other to ensure they are.

I (rather kindly) gave a line to Roger to use in his groom's speech so he could surprise everyone on the day. He concluded his speech by saying that we had started the honeymoon early and I was three months pregnant.

Now, I'm not suggesting this can easily be replicated (and it does make the dress a bit snug) but it did ensure his speech was memorable.

2 – SAY WHAT YOU SEE

My favourite brand of comedy is based on observation. It's also the easiest to master. The adage 'It's funny because it's true' makes sense.

Comedians have a skilled eye when it comes to noticing the strange things in life that we take for granted but it's often just about taking the time to look.

Everyone in this world is weird in their very own way, so get a mirror and hold it up to your relationship. Question your behaviour, habits and unwritten rules. Look at the everyday frustrations and recurring issues.

We can all relate to other people's relationships, and people appreciate it if you talk honestly about yours. Okay, not everyone's partner puts sweet chilli sauce on their toast for breakfast but everyone can appreciate having a partner with weird habits.

To make observational humour work, the trick is to be as specific as possible. Even positive qualities can be humorous if you dissect them.

Your next challenge is to think about your partner's funniest traits and find proof of them.

You did a similar challenge when thinking about stories, but this time, it's not about stand-out stories, just everyday observations.

PARTNER'S TRAITS	INSPIRATION
They're a shopaholic	They can't walk past a TK Maxx without breaking into a hot sweat ... the lure of the strip lighting and jumbled rails of ski wear pulling them in, despite the fact it's 30 degrees and we're on our way to the beach.
They're a worrier	They worry about whether we accidentally left a plug on when we go to bed at night, about a text they sent that didn't have a kiss on it, about whether Easter cards are actually a 'thing', and about whether water really can go off if it's kept in a bottle too long.
They're a hypochondriac	They visit the doctors so often that they were actually invited to their wedding.

3 – THE KILLER QUESTIONS

Whenever I work with a client, I ask the same tried and tested questions. Sometimes, there's a deafening silence, but there's generally at least a couple of questions that elicit a great response.

See how you get on ...

KILLER QUESTIONS	INSPIRATION
What are they surprisingly good at?	Surprisingly strong despite their little T-rex arms. Can open any jar, even after I secretly superglued one on.
And surprisingly bad at?	Cannot put up a tent, even those self-erecting ones.
What basic life skill are you still trying to teach them?	To use their indicator when driving. They seem to think the Highway Code is based on ESP.
What do you argue about?	When facial hair becomes a beard. Crumbs in condiments. Whether going to the hairdresser should cost more than £150.
Do you have any secret couple behaviours or rituals that no one else knows about?	On Valentine's Day we get competitive about who is the more romantic. It's like a wrestling match with flowers.
Stupid stuff they do / have ever done	Gives names to inanimate objects like Susie the Shower and Pete the Plant.
Embarrassing guilty pleasures	Loves Disneyland. Can wear the Mickey Mouse ears without a hint of irony. Has a huge amount of Disney toys that they call 'collectables'.

Continued on next page

KILLER QUESTIONS	INSPIRATION
Obsessions	They love peanut butter and will have it on anything – including pasta and salads. They love buying intellectual, worthy books that they don't actually enjoy reading.
Anything shocking or surprising about them?	They've never watched *The Lion King* and they make tea like a maniac. Milk first.
Unusual habits / behaviour	They leave teabags on the kitchen counter and always leave one bite of food on their plate (saying they're on a diet even if they've just eaten half a ton of burrito).

4 – SELF-DEPRECATION

Of course, it's not just your partner you need to be looking at . . . it's you.

Self-deprecation is a brilliant tool to utilise. Arguably the strongest, most powerful form of comedy. It's also the safest.

Sometimes, the people who you think will be good sports aren't. The only thing that's 100 per cent safe for you to take the piss out of is yourself.

Not only is it safe, it's sensible. Studies have shown that people who use self-deprecating humour are seen as more humble and consequently more emotionally intelligent and attractive. Yes, *physically* attractive.

So, if you want to come across as incredibly wise and super-hot, redo the killer questions with *you* as the target.

As Claire Wetton adds, 'Crucially, most jokes in the speech should be at the expense of the person speaking.'

Andrew Shanahan agrees: 'It's important to recognise your own absurdity.'

5 – WHEN DO THEY MAKE YOU LAUGH?

There's no bigger compliment than being able to make someone laugh, so what does your other half do that's guaranteed to give you the giggles?

Perhaps it's that weird dance they break into when they notice you're in a grump. Or their inability to remember song lyrics? Or their dedication to hiding behind a door for twenty minutes or squeezing into a cupboard just to 'boo' you.

Spend time spotting those marvellous moments when you laugh together.

Comedy techniques

Hopefully, you now have a few nuggets of comedy content to play with. Now, here's how to improve what you've got.

1 – EXAGGERATE

I spend about 200 per cent of my working life exaggerating.

It's easy and effective. Take one of the insights you've highlighted in the above exercise and now exaggerate it.

For example...

Forgetful	They forget what they're doing, while they're doing it. It's like living with that guy from *Memento*, reminders and 'to do' lists everywhere. To really freak them out, I like hiding the post-it that says 'write my to do list'.

Obsessively tidy	Man, they love dusting. People think millennials love tech but not this one. This one loves nothing more than a wet wipe. In fact, I was relieved to see they didn't put a crate of bleach on the wedding gift list.
Love interior design	Every surface in the house now has to have a diffuser on it, which if you didn't know, is a pot of smelly liquid with sticks poking out of it. They call it décor. I call it a hazard. And cushions... they're everywhere. I mean, how many bums can one couple have?

2 – BE SPECIFIC

An anecdote becomes much funnier when people can create a tangible image in their head. Detail matters.

Rather than saying your partner had a car accident as teenager, say, 'they drove their beloved Fiat Panda into the ditch in full view of the sixth form'.

3 – THE RULE OF THREE

Classic, foundation-level writing technique this one.

As Claire Wetton explains, 'It's basically two genuine examples of something, and then a funny or surprising example.'

Three just works. Think about Beyonce's 'Single Ladies' video. See. It works.

Practically, three gives the impression that you're setting up a pattern.

For example: 'We love nothing more than an evening spent

watching the ballet, or going to The Old Vic, or, more usually, slobbing out on the sofa watching *Married at First Sight, Australia.*'

4 – THE CALLBACK

> 'The callback is the ultimate comedy writer cheat code.'
>
> **ED AMSDEN AND TOM COLES**

The callback is where you plant a story or a piece of info at the start of the speech, possibly as a throwaway line, and then reference it later on. It makes it seem that you've been working up to that punchline the whole time and suggests you're smarter than you are.

For example, you tell a story about how you accidentally stapled your shoes to the floor when you were renovating your first house together. Later, you conclude your speech by saying that you can't believe your favourite person in the world will be by your side forever more, 'Even if I do have to staple their shoes to the floor.'

The callback is basically establishing an inside joke that everyone is part of.

To make it work:

1 Plant something funny, and, crucially, memorable in the first third of your speech.
2 Then simply refer to it towards the end of your speech.

Voilà. You've become a comedy pro.

5 – THE TOPPER

This is when you deliver a punchline and add on a sneaky extra follow-up. It's like having a pudding and then getting served a complimentary affogato.

It's the extra gag that keeps the laughter coming. For example ...

'I was incredibly impressed by my best man's stamina that night ... But then again, that's what crack-cocaine will do for you.

'That is a joke! Felix does not do crack-cocaine ... That I know of. I know nothing about those months he spent travelling in Bolivia last year.'

BUILDING BLOCK 4 – NAILING THE ROMANCE AND SENTIMENT

Paying a romantic tribute to your partner should be at the heart of your speech but strangely, it's something that *can* be overlooked.

One in five respondents in a Guides for Brides poll said they had witnessed a groom speech where he hadn't actually mentioned his partner beyond saying they were beautiful.

That, I'm afraid, is not on.

Your wedding is an opportunity to celebrate your partner and leave them in no doubt that you relish every pore of them.

Of course, it's hard not to resort to the obvious clichés when you talk about love – 'soulmate', 'the one', 'my best friend' – yawn, you're boring me, darling.

But you *can* be romantic, insightful and poignant without being boring, cheesy, or becoming target practice for your mates who suddenly want to chuck olives from the mezze table at you.

It's just about thinking differently.

In fact, think like a comedian. Because, in many ways, learning to be romantic is similar to learning to be funny. You can use many of the same techniques, including asking yourself some questions and simply observing your life together.

The art of being in love, and remaining in love, involves noticing the beautiful everyday things. And this chapter is going to show you how.

Why romance matters

Everyone loves love, so your challenge is to bring it to life in such a way that it ignites everyone's oxytocin.

Science proves that listening to someone talk about falling in love can make people feel like they are literally falling in love themselves.

A great wedding speech can – *should* – have the same effect as a classic romcom; releasing the pleasure hormones, dopamine and oxytocin.

People relate to other people's love stories instinctively. In fact, research has shown that when a character touches their love interest's arm in a movie, the area of your brain that interprets touch is activated, proving just how empathic humans can be.

This all goes to show that when you get to the sentimental part of the speech you are genuinely dropping a massive love-bomb on your audience, something that will have an impact on the rest of the night.

Who doesn't love a dancefloor crammed with dopamine-filled dancers?

Expert insight

'Don't assume your romantic sentiment needs to be poetic or profound. It just has to be true to you.'

ANDREW SHANAHAN

'I think it says how much speeches mean to the wedding day, and to people in general, that they're always the climax of any reality wedding show. The speeches are "the thing". It's not the ceremony, it's the speeches where people really express their emotions.'

ELEONORA TUCCI

'In the couple's speeches I want to learn something about them – either individually or as a couple. I don't want to hear "I knew Debbie was the one as soon as soon as we met" – argh, don't lie! I hate the lazy tropes.

'Sure, think about when and where the love affair started but talk about why and how was the bond formed. My partner said he knew I was the man for him when he saw me talk to topiary!'

EDUARDO BRANIFF

'To avoid clichés, don't sit down and just think you're going to type out some amazing poignant poetry. Instead, watch your partner for a couple of days and take notes. What do you love about them?'

ANNA PRICE OLSON

'Sometimes I literally google "'a different way to say I love you" and find lots of things that then trigger a new idea – like a theologian from the 1950s might have a great idea that speaks the perfect line.'

KAT WILLIAMS

'Don't bother talking about the physical attributes of your partner too much, certainly not in a serious way. People have eyes.'

ED AMSDEN AND TOM COLES

'At a big Asian wedding it's highly likely that guests will only know one half of the newlyweds and then, maybe only tenuously! Telling your love story is a great way to connect with everyone there and get people genuinely rooting for your union.'

SHAI HUSSAIN

'Remember, this is an honour, a biggie, don't phone it in with a "that will do". Give this speech a little bit of your soul.'

ANDREW SHANAHAN

'Avoid all the traditional metaphors. Instead of saying "I love you from the bottom of my heart", say "I love you even more than I love my Converse". Make it surprising.'

KAT WILLIAMS

'Men need to be comfortable with intimacy. Take the "man" out of romance. Don't be detached.'

EDUARDO BRANIFF

Romance don'ts

Do not...

- **Be generic** – If your romantic lines could be substituted into a stranger's wedding speech, well, you're doing something wrong. Romance demands that you get personal.
- **Be smug** – Being married for a few hours does not grant you the right to be a smug-married yet. Remember there's likely to be single people out there so resist the urge to suggest finding a life-partner is the only reason for living. You don't want the bridesmaids crying before 5pm!
- **Use meaningless clichés and platitudes** – Seriously, 'soulmate' is a waste of your word count. What about 'partner-in-crime' instead?
- **Overuse adjectives** – Avoid using too many adjectives and *prove*, don't tell. Use evidence to back up your claims.

Romance dos

Make sure you . . .

- **Remember romance doesn't need to be serious** – You can deliver the sweetest lines with a smile on your face.
- **Concentrate on what makes your partner unique** – The most powerful way to be romantic is finding the qualities and quirks that make your partner truly unique.

  — The truth is, nearly all the clients we work with think their other half is gorgeous, kind and generally amazing. That's the way marriage works.

  — To be *genuinely* romantic you have to hunt down the things that make your partner 'them'. Are they a tech-fiend, a gym bunny, a library lover, or the world's oldest Haribo addict? Rather than portraying them as some sort of idealistic love-god, relish who they actually *are*.

- **Tell the truth** – Seems obvious but what you say needs to be true. Wedding speakers often feel compelled to glorify their love; to exaggerate their passion, to sugar-coat the reality and, sometimes, even lie.

And what if your relationship hasn't been the traditional fairy tale one? What if you've split up a couple of times or if it took you lots of persuasion before you agreed to get married? What if you started your romance whilst married to other people?

The fact is, these things happen.

While no one wants to know about your indiscretions or doubts, it's likely that a few friends know about them and, if your partner does, you don't want them thinking you're portraying your relationship in a disingenuous way. To do so pays a disservice to the love that you have.

Allude to the challenges without spelling them out or reminding your loved one of a horrible time unnecessarily. They deserve a little bit of your soul today. Recognise your faults; be humble and vulnerable. Say 'I used to fear commitment', recognise that you've 'been an idiot' at times and then your proclamations of love seem all the more genuine.

Romantic hackathon

Okay, this is the bit where you pretend you're part of a hot-shot, sexy CSI team and you're gathering evidence, but instead of sentencing the guilty party to a life behind bars, you're sentencing them to a life married to you.

Trust me, this is more romantic than it sounds.

Work through the next set of questions and you'll find it easier to fish out these little romantic nuggets.

What you want is that 'on-the-sofa' style romance. Sometimes it's the smallest embers that build the most beautiful flames.

1 – ROMANTIC MOMENTS

Drill down to those moments of romance that have delighted you over the years . . .

PROMPT	INSPIRATION
When you started to fancy them	On our first date, I felt that thing everyone had been talking about for years but I'd never really understood. That spark. That excitement. That afterglow the following morning; the sense that my life had changed. Finally I got it . . . love. And so I text them at 6am to say 'Is it too soon to ask for a second date?'

PROMPT	INSPIRATION
When you fell in love	I didn't actually notice I'd fallen in love until my mum told me. She looked at me one day, as I watched you in the garden, and she smiled. 'You're in love,' she said. And she was right.
When you knew you wanted to marry them	They told me that they didn't have wrinkles because they had decided, aged ten, that they didn't want them and had made a deliberate effort never to frown.

I thought to myself, that is the kind of dedication I want in a partner; someone who can go through life, choosing never to frown. |
| Your favourite memories | We've been lucky enough to do lots of exciting things over the years – from paragliding in Italy to climbing to the peak of the Leshan Giant Buddha despite a fear of heights. But one moment stands out to me. It was a friend's birthday party in a dodgy bar. It was loud, it was crowded, and I was speaking to someone I hardly knew. Then, I looked up and saw them watching me from the other side of the bar. |

PROMPT	INSPIRATION
	We didn't say a word but we looked at each other across the madness, and we knew. It's a look that I will remember for the rest of my life.
Your best day together	In a crowded, chaotic world, it's them who brings me peace and makes my soul content. We ended the day having fish and chips in a bus shelter, shielding from the rain and the 45mph winds. It was cold, getting dark and we didn't know how we were getting home. But then I realised I was having one of my best days ever and I thought … that's something to do with the person beside me.

2 – YOUR PARTNER'S POSITIVE TRAITS

Think of three wonderful adjectives to describe your partner and find the evidence to prove them.

We've done a similar exercise before, but here we're focusing on your partner's most brilliant characteristics.

(If your partner is …) Thoughtful	(If your partner is …) Fun	(If your partner is …) Caring
Secretly learnt to make my gran's rice pudding recipe as a special treat for me.	They put on the most extravagant parties – even for our cats, as many of you know having recently partied at Pussy-fest.	When my dad was ill, they visited him every day. They were kind, caring and … couldn't resist kicking his ass at chess. Of course, my dad loved it and the joy they brought him is something I'll always be thankful for.
Picked me up at 1am from the station after I thought I'd lost my wallet on a night out and didn't call me an idiot when I found it in my jacket the next morning.	They're dedicated to getting a laugh. Will think nothing of spending a month making a fancy dress outfit or making a birthday video for a friend that involves 10 hours of filming and 12 evenings of editing.	Completely changed their birthday plans when they discovered my sister didn't like heights. Yes, the original plan was to go on the country's longest, fastest zip wire – so think yourself lucky sis!
Secretly ordered a bag of that overpriced coffee that I happened to mention I loved, only to discover it was a giant 10 kg bag that is now having to be stored in our oven. They admitted it was rather expensive!	Will always be first up at the karaoke bar 'just to get things going' despite knowing they can't sing a note.	They can't resist a sickly or lost animal. Our house has turned into an unlicensed zoo. It smells, they're expensive, but then I watch them cuddling up to the cats and I see they were designed to care.

A good way to package a list like this is to bookend it with some humour.

For example, 'If I've had a stressful day at work, they run me a bath. If I can't buy my favourite brand of coffee, they find out a way to import it. If my car is looking scruffy, they secretly get it valeted. Do you know how hard it is to live with someone this perfect?!'

3 – THE 'LIKE LIST'

This is distinct from what you love about your partner. Sometimes love can be highly subjective and intangible, while *liking* someone is all about them being a certifiable decent human being.

For example, today I like my partner because he let me have the last bagel, chose not to make a big deal about the fact I was wrong, made me laugh, picked up some litter without moaning about it and knew a lot of random facts about space that genuinely blew my mind.

Sometimes 'I like' sounds more powerful in a wedding speech because it's less expected than 'I love'.

I used this technique in my own wedding speech. 'I like how you make me playlists and I like that you bring me a tea in the morning. I like how you introduced me to camping and I like how you understand pensions. I like that you're a great friend to everyone you love and I really like you in your olive-green T-shirt. In short, I like you a lot and I'm so incredibly grateful that the feeling seems mutual.'

A decade later, friends still mention the olive-green T-shirt line.

So . . . **what do you like about your partner?**

Write your list and pick the best.

4 – THE CUTE QUESTION

No matter how serious your partner is, no matter if they're a chief exec of a multinational, I hope you still find them cute.

Maybe your guests should know about the daft one-sided conversations you hear them having with the dog in the mornings. Or perhaps their morning ritual of 'lazy yoga' is one of their quirks that you've grown to love.

When do you find your partner cute?

5 – LOVE COMPARISONS

Comparing your partner to the *other* things you love in life is a simple way to say 'I love you' with a bit of weight behind it.

So think, what *else* do you love?

'More than' inspiration

I love you more than . . .

- YouTube videos of sneezing pandas.
- Krispy Kreme doughnuts.
- Finding vintage Chanel on eBay.
- Impressive Wordle stats.
- A Barack Obama, Chris Martin and Jerry Seinfeld hybrid.

I mean, who wouldn't be overwhelmed by a declaration of love like that?

6 – PROMISES

Remember when Jennifer told Brad she'd always make him his favourite banana milkshake and he vowed to split the difference on the thermostat? Okay, we all know how that marriage ended but the original thinking was pretty cool.

Why not incorporate some bespoke promises into your speech?

'I promise' inspiration

- To always protect you from spiders. Even the tiny ones. Even the ones in your dreams that come out of the walls.
- To console you whenever your team crashes out of the tournament. *(Whisper to your guests) A lot.*
- Never to watch an episode of *The Mandalorian* without you.
- To learn to make your favourite carrot cake.
- To learn to stack the dishwasher properly.

---

7 – COUNTER-INTUITIVE ROMANCE

The secret to a good marriage is finding someone who knows you're not perfect but treats you like you are.

And sometimes listing the minor foibles and irritations can be used to good effect.

So what are the things that bug you about your partner?

'Real love' inspiration

- I love you. Sure, you can't eat anything without dropping crumbs on the floor and you manage to spoil most movies by correctly guessing the ending, but the truth is, I want to spend every irritating minute of my life with you.
- You talk about Elon Musk far too much, you always leave your trainers in the hall and you still put wrapping paper in the recycling even though I've told you not to a thousand times. But if you didn't exist, I'd miss all that.
- These days, I *need* to know what Elon Musk is thinking, I *need* to trip over your shoes in the hall, and I *need* to check for non-recyclables in the recycling bin. Basically, I need you in my life.
- I never thought I'd marry someone who slept with the window open in winter. I never thought I'd be with someone who could ignore texts for a whole day before responding. And I never imagined I'd be in a relationship with someone who insisted on camping holidays or enjoyed listening to Mozart. But then again, I hadn't met you.

---

8 – SELF-DEPRECATING PROCLAMATION

Being open and honest can be remarkably powerful. In fact, the research professor Brené Brown's talk about her research into the power of vulnerability has now amassed 50 million views, making it one of the most popular TED Talks ever.

Of course, it can't be forced or 'put on' to be meaningful. It has to be authentic.

It also has to be on the right side of pathetic. Divulging how you used to drink too much and sleep with completely inappropriate people whilst you searched for true love is not the sort of vulnerability we're after here.

But what can you be open and honest about (that won't scare people)?

'Vulnerable' inspiration

- After two failed marriages, I started to think that maybe marriage isn't for me. That maybe I'm one of those renegades who just do better on their own. I'd got used to an empty house. I was happy going to parties by myself. I even started playing golf. And then, they came and blew away all my plans in an instant.

- I never thought I could find someone who I could sit with on the sofa, without makeup, in my slobbiest joggers, and they'd still fancy me. I mean, they're weird.

- My parents have had the best marriage. A truly equal, fun-loving, supportive union. Even as a child, I knew they were incredibly lucky to have that, and I never thought I'd find that for myself. I mean, it defies the odds, right? Simple statistics says, not a chance. But now, I'm up for the gamble. Now, I feel ready to take on the system and beat the odds.

---

9 – KILLER LINES

Killer lines aren't for everyone. For some people, a killer line will feel too much of a romantic leap, too far removed from your normal self – maybe, even, a bit cheesy.

But give it a go.

A killer line is the romantic sentence (or two) that will bring people to their knees. The line they will quote back to you later at the bar. The one that your partner will want to get printed and framed and put on your living room wall.

So try to think BIG about what love means to you.

'Killer' inspiration

- I will try to surprise you, and remind you when you least expect it, how wonderful you are.
- When I met you, I discovered you are never too old to find a dream.
- What makes a life rich is the people you share it with.
- Sometimes a moment is enough to make a life worth living. And this is such a moment. If I never again feel as happy as this moment, and I hope I do, well, this is still enough.
- When you look for a partner, don't look at what they do for a living or how much they have in the bank, look at how they treat their family and friends. Are they loving to their gran? Do they listen to their father? Do they stand up for the people they love? If the answer is yes, they're worth holding on to.
- I thought I was happy before we met, but actually, I had no idea. I look back at my life before you and I wonder what made me smile. You brought colour to my life that I didn't even know existed.

BUILDING BLOCK 5 (THE CHEAT'S BUILDING BLOCK) – QUOTES

Plagiarism isn't allowed but quoting clever people is.

Quotes are a great way of nailing the romantic bit of your speech without it being cringey or clichéd. It's also an easy way to add a laugh without resorting to a wedding gag.

How to use quotes

MAKE THE QUOTES MEANINGFUL

Think about the songs, the films, the books that mean something to you both. Do any of these lend themselves to a great quote?

If you're both bookworms, check out your bookshelves. If you're festival lovers or Sonos-swingers, pick your favourite tracks and see what lines you can find lurking in the melody.

Or maybe you both love a romantic film. Clearly, *The Notebook* has plenty to steal from!

DON'T OVERLOAD YOUR SPEECH WITH QUOTES

One ideally. Two maximum. One at the top and one towards the end.

QUOTE RECOGNISABLE NAMES (OR AT LEAST PROVIDE SOME CONTEXT)

It's always good to quote people you've actually heard of (or at least respect after you've looked them up on Wikipedia).

You'll find there's loads of great quotes by people you've never heard of, but do you really want to qualify them by saying they were written by a 'relationship consultant'?

DON'T JUST USE QUOTES FOR THE SENTIMENTAL BIT

You don't just need to quote philosophers or romantic poets. You can quote comedians and musicians too.

ADD A BACK REFERENCE

Put the quote into a personal context, or make it humorous with a suitable 'ad lib'.

Quote inspiration

Okay, this time you *can* google.

- **Children's books** – A surprisingly good source of poignant quotes. Think about your personal favourites but I find *Winnie the Pooh*, Charlie Brown and Dr Seuss brilliant.
- **Rom-coms** – *When Harry Met Sally*, *The Notebook*, *Brief Encounter*, *Father of the Bride*, *Sleepless in Seattle*, *Good Will Hunting*, *Eternal Sunshine of the Spotless Mind*; these are just a few films that include classic lines. Hunt your own.
- **Music** – This is incredibly personal but I'm a fan of the lyrics of The Smiths, Foo Fighters, Bon Iver, and, being Scottish, The Proclaimers' 'I'm Gonna Be (500 Miles)'.
- **Philosophers** – Plato, Jean-Paul Sartre, Voltaire, Socrates, Proust, Aristotle, Lao Tzu, Nietzsche, Euripides, Alain de Botton are a good starting point.
- **Religious texts** – If it truly speaks to you.
- **Authors** – So many to choose from! F. Scott Fitzgerald, Paulo Coelho, Sylvia Plath, C. S. Lewis, Louis de Bernières, Leo Tolstoy, Emily Brontë, Nicholas Sparks, Oscar Wilde, John Green, Maya Angelou and Zelda Fitzgerald are a few of my favs.
- **Comedians** – Jerry Seinfeld, Tina Fey, Will Ferrell, Rob Delaney, Mindy Kaling. Consider classic comedians like George Burns, Rita Rudner and Phyllis Diller too.
- **Politicians and notable figures** – Einstein, Michelle Obama, Vincent Van Gogh, Audrey Hepburn, Winston Churchill, Frida Kahlo, Queen Elizabeth II. A historical icon instantly adds weight to your words.

I hope this has given you an idea of the variety of sources where you can find great quotes.

And, if all else fails . . . search Pinterest for marriage or love quotes!

Stage 2 recap

Etiquette
- Modern etiquette is about being polite and thoughtful, not being overly formal.
- Don't feel you need to thank everyone, just the important people.
- Don't give gifts during the speeches.
- Keep toasts to a minimum.
- Carefully consider how you can honour the dearly departed outside of the speech as well as within it.

Story-hunting
- Stories don't need to be about momentous events, they can simply be used as an illustration of your life together.
- The cornerstones of your relationship (meeting, falling in love, moving in together) are a good place to start when story-hunting.
- Once you gather your stories, see if you can identify a common theme running through any of them.

Finding your funny
- Avoid generic gags at all costs.
- Observation is key to wedding speech humour. Watch your relationship dynamic for a week and comedy will come to you.
- Include self-deprecation.
- Avoid anything that could possibly offend anyone.

Nailing the romance

- State facts, not fiction; relish the person you're marrying rather than an idealised, photoshopped version of them.
- Don't try to be poetic or profound if this doesn't come naturally to you. Aim for cute and insightful instead.
- Wrap up your romance with humour. It helps it stand out more.

Use quotes sparingly

SPEECH INSPIRATION

Groom speech – Delivered by Kanav
Background: Kanav has married Priyanka. They live in Nottingham, England and are of South Asian descent. Kanav is an architect. The wedding is traditionally large, with over 350 people attending.

Ladies and gentlemen, uncles and aunties, *bhaiyon aur behano*, boys and girls – namaste and welcome. My wife and I . . . (*pause for applause*) thank you so much for coming to share this wonderful weekend with us.

Of course, as much as we'd love to take credit for it, this has been a mammoth group effort with so many to thank for their involvement. After this, our parents are going to take a well-earned rest and sort out the global warming issue.

Now, you already heard the disastrous way Priyanka and I met from the best man, so I won't go over that again. But it's true what he said – we were . . . well, we *are* like chalk and cheese. Or some would say coal and paneer. And you can tell which one of us is paneer, can't you?

As a primary school teacher, Priyanka is warm, caring,

communicative – a real people's person who works amongst a number of impatient clients every day. As an architect, I'm concise, introverted, and analytical – I need my space to focus on just one project, sometimes for months at a time. Basically, I'm boring, slow and don't like hanging out with people.

(*Look around*) Really, I've no idea how this all happened.

But, as the saying goes, opposites attract and you can see that for yourselves in our wedding. Priyanka's creativity and vivid imagination have gone wild. Getting married in October, she actually wanted this weekend to have a Halloween-themed twist, asking guests to wear Indian costumes, but ripped and bloodied so we'd all look like zombies.

At one point, there was even a Thriller dance routine being planned.

I, of course, shot down idea after idea with my pragmatism, wanting us to keep things traditional, low-maintenance and on the right side of sane. But, if any of you want to rip up your lehangas and kurtas and cover yourselves in the madras, feel free. Though, looking at my mother, maybe not!

Of course, I couldn't reject *all* of Priyanka's inspired ideas and you'll spot many of them here this evening: the Indian food twists on pizzas and sushi, and the dosa-crepe stand were all her idea. The games of Antakshari, the carrom tournament, the masala cocktails and the band that does rock covers of Bollywood numbers? All her.

Whilst she came up with all the cool ideas, I kept in my lane; compiling an Excel spreadsheet and making sure we could actually pay for it all. And when I say '*we*', what I actually mean is we pay a small percentage while our parents pay the rest. Thank you Maa, Papa, Saasuma, Sasurji. We owe you. Literally!

But honestly, watching Priyanka plan our wedding has been an absolute joy and seeing how beautiful she looks today is truly humbling.

Priyanka's knowledge and creativity as a teacher, even as an individual, have never failed to astound me. I had no idea how much my life lacked colour until I met her. She introduced me to different foods, different countries and cultures, and even different films and TV.

I honestly thought she was ready to break up with me when I told her I'd never watched *Kuch Kuch Hota Hain*. And I was sure it was the end of us when she forced me to watch *Maine Pyar Kiya* and I walked out halfway through the film. Those of you who don't know, she loves *Maine Pyar Kiya* the same way I love KFC.

As I say, opposites attract.

Priyanka brings the fun and the excitement to the relationship, and I hope, as an architect, I bring the structure. It may not sound as fun as colour, but when you build the foundations of a relationship you need *both* passion and pragmatism to keep it from crumbling when confronted with life's challenges.

We visit monuments like the Taj Mahal and the Pyramids of Giza because of their colour and the emotions they evoke, and thankfully they continue to stand due to their intelligent architecture. Both foundation and beauty play equally important roles in maintaining the immortality of these international treasures. And I think it's the same principle that means Priyanka and I will stand the test of time.

We bring out the best in each other and push one another to challenge the people we are. Sure, this can lead to a few 'debates' but we're ready to hear each other out, and most importantly, we're ready to compromise. This wedding is the perfect example of the beauty that compromise can lead to. I've no doubt we have a few more disagreements ahead of us, but I'm equally sure that our compromises will lead to ever more beautiful times shared together.

Priyanka, before I met you, I already had strong foundations. In fact, I was an unmovable object, working in the same place I'd joined since graduation, living in the same flat. You came in like an unstoppable rainbow grenade, and I don't think my life was ever the same again. I don't want my life to ever be the same again.

Whenever you're about, *Kuch Kuch Hota Hain* (something happens) and it's fair to say, *Maine Pyar Kiya* (I fell in love).

Now, if you can all join me in a toast to my beautiful wife, my very own rainbow grenade, my wonderful Priyanka.

To Priyanka.

WRITTEN BY SHAI HUSSAIN

Gay bride speech – Delivered by Cassidy
Background: Cassidy has married Mia. They live in Florida. Cassidy is 30 and Mia is 47. Mia is a surfing instructor.

Good evening everyone – on behalf of my wife and I (*pause for applause*), I wanted to say a few words before the meal is served, to tell you how much we love you all.

A wedding is a time to celebrate love and, primarily, we think of that as being the love between the couple getting married.

Mia and I think it's wider than that though; we think it's also about celebrating the love from and to everyone here. The love that exists between the people you know. The love that could exist between the people you don't.

Today is not just our wedding, it's a celebration of that love.

There's too much darkness in the world and so today at our wedding you have just one challenge: find that love. Squeeze that hand. Pinch that ass. Kiss those lips.

I've never been in love before. I loved my parents and my brothers, but that wasn't really a love that I ever discovered. It was just always there. It was like oxygen. No one is surprised that they can breathe, it's just this vital component of our lives that exists all around us from the very second we're born.

Falling in love with Mia was like discovering this part of me that had always existed, but I'd just never known about before. Like one day I'd woken up and found that I had three arms. Or that I could speak another language. To borrow a metaphor from Mia's favourite film *The Matrix*, it was like I was Neo getting plugged into the Matrix and suddenly I knew kung-fu.

Realising I loved Mia shocked me.

I've found being in love hard. I know that sounds crazy, but when I uncovered this wonderful new thing, I spent a long time being scared that I might lose it. I spent even longer being scared that Mia might not love me. I'm angry at that fear I felt, because it wasted time and, as with all fear, it never actually changed anything.

I will always remember the moment when Mia agreed to give me surfing lessons. I'd surfed since I was three and competed in a few local championships, but when I saw that Mia was offering lessons, I conveniently forgot all about that and she took me on as what she thought was an eager apprentice.

In our second lesson the waves were all choppy and foam. We were waiting in the surf for a decent set to come in and our boards were touching. Mia raised herself up on her board and asked me how long I'd surfed for. At that point, several lies queued up on my tongue, but I found myself telling her the truth. She laughed and said she was still going to charge me for the lessons.

We went for a drink later that day and I explained to Mia that I'd not known how to get to spend time with her and I tried to convince her that I wasn't weird. Typical Mia, she ignored what I was saying with a wave of her hand and kissed me. We've been together ever since.

Find that love, people.

Occasionally, people ask me if it bothers me that Mia is older than me and I tell them that I've never noticed. The honest truth is that I think it's strange that people feel that there's an age that you can love. If you're 29, you can only love a 29-year-old? People in their forties have to love people in their forties? Why?

It's not about an age, it's about love, and Mia is the love that found me. If I shut myself off to that because of a number, then that is disrespectful to love. If love finds you, you welcome it in, it doesn't matter about numbers or colours or sizes, it's love!

I promised myself, and Mia, that I wouldn't speak for too long today. I want to thank our parents and families for joining us on this day. We love you and we want you to feel that viscerally.

To our friends, we want you to know that we feel the love from you, and we are reflecting that back to you. We also want to thank love for being here in this place today and for filling our hearts with this amazing oxygen, this beautiful new arm, this incredible kung-fu – we have found you and we are not letting go!

Ladies and gentlemen, please stand and raise your glasses. Here's to finding that love.

WRITTEN BY ANDREW SHANAHAN

Bride speech – Delivered by Nicole
Background: Nicole has married Adama. They live in Chicago and met at church.

Good afternoon, ladies and gentlemen. It's my absolute honour and privilege to welcome you to our special day. A day made all the more special for us by your presence.

Now, in life, people say 'God works in mysterious ways', and never has that been truer than in our relationship. When you think about God having a romantic plan for you, you think of Cupid's arrow striking you in the heart as a tall, dark stranger saunters into your life. Whereas what I got was an awkward guy in his dad's suit walking into church and tripping over a mop bucket.

So, sure he probably wasn't the inspiration for Christian Gray, but actually the *deeply* embarrassing trip over a mop bucket caused me to check if he was okay, which led to us sitting next to each other, and which led to us having a conversation. Admittedly that conversation was throughout the entire service . . . sorry, Pastor Watkins.

Yet in that chance conversation, we found out one thing, one thing that has stood us in good stead ever since: That we share a lot in common. Sure, I *also* found out he likes pineapple on his pizza, but you can't win them all.

Hideous taste in pizza aside, we talked for hours about our favorite films, music and our deep love of gaming. Side note: for a man of God, I'm not quite sure why he chose the PlayStation screen-name 'DemonBoy666'.

But as much as there was an immediate bond between us, there wasn't yet a romantic one. As before, God didn't make his plan immediately obvious. Instead of presenting it in one go, fully wrapped with a nice little bow, he gave it to us in pieces. Bit by bit, allowing us to piece it together like a jigsaw where the full picture is obscured until the last piece is placed.

We stayed friends for three years, staying up late, gaming together and talking about the world and our plans. Both oblivious to the fact we'd be stood here, getting married five years later.

Although it does seem that our friends *weren't* oblivious, as unbeknownst to us, they'd begun taking bets on a 'when will Nicole and Adama go on their first date' sweepstake. Well, that was the PG version of the bet anyway. The R-rated version isn't one I care to repeat in a house of God.

But soon, this plan would start to reveal itself to Adama and I. I've always said, I knew there was a spark between us when Adama gently held my hand to guide me round a puddle. Although I asked Adama when *he* knew that he was attracted to me and he said, 'That night you wore that see-through top to the gym.' So maybe it wasn't all as romantic as I first thought.

But, whether it was a puddle or a see-through top, the final piece of the jigsaw was set in place. And from there on out, it was plain sailing. We were friends who already knew everything about each other . . . I say that, he did recently admit to me that his favorite film isn't *Citizen Kane*, it's actually *The Fast and the Furious: Tokyo Drift*. Which admittedly did make me question this whole 'God's plan' thing . . . And the whole 'wedding thing'.

But what I'm saying is, our story wasn't some huge fairy tale, birds tweeting, love-at-first-sight kinda deal. It was a slow, cautious build up, which isn't stereotypically romantic, but has enabled us to create a solid, unshakeable foundation that our future can be built on.

Friends first. Partners second. Now that's a plan I can get behind.

While I have you here, I'd like to take this opportunity to offer some words of thanks to some incredibly special people. Although I warn you, between Adama and I, we have over a dozen siblings to thank, so this might take a while. (*Look to the back of the room*) Lock the doors.

Firstly, to my mom and dad. They have taught me everything I know about life and love. Smart, caring, thoughtful . . . and dad's okay as well. From being a young child, I have been around a couple that work as a team and are stronger than their parts. So, if in marriage, Adama and I even have 10 per cent of what you both have, I know we'll be in a good place.

To Adama's mom, Michelle. A bold, kind woman who managed to bring up seven children, mostly on her own. You've been a great source of strength and support for me throughout my time with Adama, and I can't wait for us to spend more time together.

Now, I can't thank all of our siblings individually, as we've only got this place booked until midnight, but I speak for both of us when I say how integral to our lives you've been, and how important you are to us both. I say that partly because I mean it, but also because you're the keepers of our most embarrassing secrets.

I want to say a special thank-you to my sister, Julia. As many of you may know, she passed away last year from cancer. Which makes today especially hard, as I couldn't ever have imagined getting married without her by my side. But while she's not here with us in person, she's here with us in every smile, every dance move and every hug. She's here with us in our and mom's filthy laugh. So, Julia, we love you and miss you, but we'll never forget you.

And finally, I want to say a thank-you to Adama. A person who has enriched my life in almost every way since stumbling into it, all those years ago. I love how you're equally happy playing games together as you are on an expensive holiday. I don't know if you remember, but when we first started dating, you made me a promise: You promised that no matter what happens you'll always be my friend.

So, DemonBoy666, I'd like to close this speech by making you a promise in return:

Our relationship started with kicking a bucket, so my promise to you is that I'll stay by your side until we kick a different bucket entirely.

Now, if you could all be upstanding and raise a toast to friends, family and loved ones.

To loved ones.

SPEECH WRITTEN BY ED AMSDEN AND TOM COLES

Stage 3 – Write Your Speech

So, we've done the hunter-gatherer stage. Now this chapter is all about curating your content and deciding on your speech narrative.

It's time to figure out the message you want to convey and select the relevant stories that illustrate the point.

As Anna Price Olson explains, 'Writing a wedding speech should be approached in the same way you would a business presentation or a university thesis. You need to consider the fundamental building blocks you want to cover. Then, work out your thesis statement, present that at the top, and go about proving it in the rest of the speech with examples and personal stories that support and reiterate your thesis throughout.'

The hardest part of writing your speech is coming up with that central thesis idea.

There's lots of terms for this – the narrative hook, the story-theme – but it's that central idea that flows through your speech and brings together all the different elements.

It's what stops your speech from being a list of random insights and anecdotes and transforms it into something more meaningful.

Once we figure out your speech theme, we'll move on to the different elements of the speech and lead you through the full writing process.

The plan

Step 1 – Find your theme

- Pick your best material.
- Look at speech themes in action. Consider what you can do with your discarded material.

Step 2 – Structure and write your speech

- Consider the ideal speech length.
- Develop the cornerstones of your speech – i.e. the start, middle and end.
- Write your toast.
- Look at joint and rhyming speeches.

Step 3 – Edit your speech

EXPERT INSIGHT

'When we write, we start with the best stories. We hunt out three or four anecdotes and just slap them down on the page. We then find a theme or a link joining them together – whether it's always being late or always thinking you're right – you have to try to link all the stories together with a thread. It's that magic thread that makes the speech work.'

ED AMSDEN AND TOM COLES

'I always start my speeches with a theme. I start by deciding what lasting impression I want everyone to be left with and I work from there.

'For grooms or brides giving a speech, I'd suggest you draw on your joint history and use this to help create a lesson or hope about your future.

'As a guest, I don't want you to tell me about your fabulous holidays or a great night out you had, tell me something that has a point to it. Every story needs to have a meaning, or at least lead to a meaning.'

EDUARDO BRANIFF

'At this stage, you might have lots of notes and ideas. Now you have to narrow it down to just the few crucial points you want to make and work out the order.

'Use the journalistic principle, "don't get it right, get it written". Once you get it written you can worry about getting it right.'

ANDREW SHANAHAN

'When I write I imagine I'm writing to the one person who needs to hear it, rather than speaking to all of my followers at once. You can't try to please everyone all the time because then it can become meaningless if you sanitise it for the sake of others. Write for your partner and then it's more likely everyone else will appreciate it too.'

KAT WILLIAMS

'I actually always start with the first sentence when I'm writing but I always have a plan. I know the overall theme of the speech, but that's where I start, literally, the start.'

CLAIRE WETTON

'How do I start a speech? I start with a blank mind in bed in the morning. So, find your thinking space, somewhere you have a clear mind and can think properly.

'If I was starting a speech I'd ask myself "What would people want to know?". Then I'd mind map it. I'd put my central theme in the middle and then have offshoots all connected to that theme.'

ALISON HARGREAVES

STEP 1 – FIND YOUR THEME

Select your best content

Okay, you've got your stash of stories, now what are you going to do with them?

Well, you pick the best and bin the rest.

You're looking for three things:

- The funniest, most entertaining stories.
- Stories that make a point (either funny or poignant).
- And a thread that connects them all.

A speech generally needs three good stories. Sometimes it only needs one. Occasionally four but very rarely.

Kat Williams adds, 'Remember, you don't need to list everything you've ever done. This is not an obituary.'

You might think your stories are so good, you can just condense each one and fit in more but it doesn't work. Good stories deserve good storytelling. They need to be built up. Pictures need to be imagined and people need time to digest the point.

So let's start by finding your theme.

Pick your theme

Some writers call it the 'throughline'. It's the thing that connects all the stories, insights, compliments and thank-yous so they sound like they work together rather than just being a rather arbitrary list of thoughts.

Some of you will already know the message you want your speech to give. In which case, work out the best stories and lines that illustrate this point.

If you haven't yet worked out your message, do it the other way round. Pick out a few of your favourite anecdotes and see if you can spot a theme that connects them.

There are infinite theme ideas but here's a few classics you could consider . . .

THEME IDEAS BASED ON YOUR RELATIONSHIP

- **Love lessons.** What you've learnt from each other over the years; the good, the bad and the plain ugly. A theme like this is great for starting with comedic examples and moving on to more profound ones.
- **Why opposites attract.** A theme that can be utilised by most couples.
- **The power of serendipity.** This works if luck has played a part in your relationship (even if it was simply that your partner lived within a 20km radius of your online dating search).
- **How love changes with time.** This is a good concept if you're getting married at a later stage in life. It can include comedic insights ('Less podium dancing, more pension haggling') but conclude with a more meaningful sentiment. ('When you get to your sixties, you know what's important to you and you can promise things that you only now truly understand.')
- **A very modern fairy tale.** This theme allows you to contrast your relationship with the traditional old-fashioned idea of love. It actually works for most relationships. Contrast where you met (online, at the pub?) with where Cinderella met her Prince

Charming, or the reality of your dating life with that of the classic Disney version.

- **The international language of love.** A great theme if you have an international guestlist. Use proverbs and words from their countries of origin to punctuate your speech. Say it in your guest's native language and then translate. It makes everyone feel included in the speech and also brings something new to the table. There are some great proverbs out there, from Ethiopia's 'Coffee and love taste better when they're hot' to India's 'It is love that makes the impossible, possible'.

THEME BASED ON YOUR PARTNER'S TRAITS

This theme can be really simple to pull off.

Think of one of your partner's most defining traits. Are they a foodie? A bit of a geek? Accident prone?

You've already done the hard work identifying these traits in action, so you have a ready-made narrative. Now all you have to do is to conclude your story by saying that, not only do you now accept this questionable quality, you fully embrace it.

THEME BASED ON THE BIG QUESTIONS

Your theme could be framed as a question that you pose at the start of your speech and then attempt to answer.

For example . . .

- Today I'm going to address the elephant in the room . . . How the hell did I manage to land such a fox?
- So, what is love? Philosophers and poets have been attempting to answer that one for years. But now . . . it's *my* turn!
- Some people think the concept of marriage is outdated. The statistics don't do it any favours. So why the heck have we just said 'I do'? Well, let me tell you . . .

You can think of even more personal questions to pose.

THEME BASED ON A SHOWSTOPPER

Find a theme by thinking about how you'd like to *end* your speech. What's your showstopping conclusion?

I'm generally not a fan of props but I do like a big idea. So, can you conclude your speech by presenting your partner with something meaningful and utterly surprising?

Not a standard present (that would be weird) but something that shows you 'get' them.

For example, present them with your attempt to recreate that amazing cake you shared on your first date.

Or, instead of your partner, surprise your guests. If your theme has been about being lucky in love, reveal to your guests that their wedding favours are, in fact, lottery tickets and that you hope they're as lucky in life as you have been.

Themes in action

Let's say you've opted for **love lessons.** You could structure your content like this:

- **Hello and welcome.**
- **Set up the theme idea:** 'Getting married is a big deal and I've learnt so much over the last year. Who knew there were twelve different shades of lemon to debate? Or that a chair becomes double the hire price if a wedding guest's bum's sitting on it? I've also learnt a fair bit about my partner too: turns out, he loves a spreadsheet. Multiple tabs, colour-coded; it was a thing of beauty and I wasn't allowed anywhere near it. But that's the thing with Ryan, he constantly surprises me and I continue to learn new things about him every day.'
- **Example 1:** The early days – 'One of the first things I learnt about him was he isn't much of a genius. As many of you know,

we met working at the Apple Store when I was an Apple Concierge and he was an Apple Genius. Supposedly.

In an attempt to get to know him better I invited him to our local pub quiz. (*Pause, look at Ryan and shake head*) Not a clue. He wouldn't accept that whales are mammals, not fish, and refused to believe the capital of Australia was somewhere he'd never heard of. He couldn't even name one Ed Sheeran song. I was embarrassed I'd invited him.'

- **Example 2:** Moving in together – 'Moving in together was also a bit of a lesson. Basically, this man cannot be trusted with a hammer. He can only be trusted to sit beside me and hand me things whilst I Do-It-Myself. Even then he's not quite sure what a nut or a bolt is.'

- **Example 3:** Day-to-day life – 'Of course, I've learnt all manner of amazing things about Ryan over the years too. I've learnt he's willing to share his body heat when I get into bed with freezing feet and an even colder nose. I've learnt he's a loving grandson and an amazing godfather to two children he adores. I've learnt he's better at folding and packing than Marie Kondo, and yes, I confess, is much neater than me.'

- **Summary:** 'Most of all, I've learnt one very important lesson and that's how to love someone with all my heart and soul.'

- **Thank-yous:** 'Over the years, I've also learnt that Ryan and I share an important quality, and that's how much we value our friends and family.' Specific thank-yous.

- **Acknowledgement of the dearly departed (if necessary).**

- **Address your partner with a final romantic tribute.**

- **Toast:** 'To love and learning'.

If you want to **focus on your partner's traits**, you could actually make it subversive:

- **Hello and welcome.**
- **Set up the theme idea:** 'Now, for you who haven't noticed, my new spouse is not only gorgeous but really incredibly loud. We will not be needing the microphone for her speech. In fact, I think our evening guests will get to hear it. But today, rather than tell you about all the times my wife has hijacked the karaoke, or told an embarrassing story rather too loudly or been asked to be quiet in a public space, I'm going to tell you about the times that they were quiet . . .'
- **Example 1:** Story from first date – 'We talked about culture, politics, even a bit about philosophy. I remember being struck by how refined and demure she was. She asked insightful questions and listened to me as if she was genuinely interested in what I had to say. Then we ordered a second glass of wine and the real Ava appeared . . .'
- **Example 2:** Story from your first holiday – 'It was the first time we'd been together 24/7 for five days solid. My ears needed a break so we decided to go diving and have a nice meditative swim underwater. Twenty minutes in, Ava sees a moderately large fish, swims to the surface and screams her head off for a solid five minutes. The instructor got his harpoon out, people on the shore were panicking and all over a rather pathetic parrotfish.'
- **Example 3:** Watching her first day as a mum – 'She was literally dumbstruck with love. When Arlo was awake, she'd just stare at him. When he was asleep, she didn't move a muscle in case he woke up. It really was a magical time, that baby bubble, but, also, shockingly quiet. A week later, of course, it was an altogether different matter! Arlo discovered his lungs, and Ava rediscovered her voice. Especially, it seemed, when a nappy needed changing.'
- **Summary:** 'I hope when I die my eardrums are burst and broken because that will mean I've spent a happy lifetime with the loudest and loveliest person I know.'

- **Acknowledgement of the dearly departed (if necessary).**
- **Address your partner with a final romantic tribute.**
- **Toast:** 'To a life lived at 120 decibels'.

If you opt to use a **question** theme, you could structure it like this...

- **Hello and welcome.**
- **Set up the theme idea:** 'Now, you know me as a lawyer. A person who believes in evidence and the power of proof. So why exactly have I just signed a contract that signs me up to something as bewildering as a lifetime of commitment? Well, let me tell you ...'
- **Evidence 1:** For example, 'Noah makes me laugh every day. Sometimes I don't want to laugh – like the time he told me to ingratiate myself with his Irish family by welcoming them with a "Pog mo thoin", basically telling his dad to kiss my ass – but I can't deny Noah has added more laughter to my life than I deserve.'
- **Evidence:** 'He's also surprisingly caring. Mostly about the Formula 1 results and pointless Twitter debates, but also about me, his family and, rather unexpectedly, small mammals.

   'I've lost count of the times he's stopped the car to help an injured badger or fox but I think it goes to show how considerate and loving he is. Admittedly, half the time, he has to bash the poor animal over the head and put an end to its suffering but still ... he's a killer who cares.'
- **Evidence 3:** 'The final proof I needed before agreeing to a lifetime of commitment, came on a very average walk we took through Westridge woods just over a year ago. I got distracted taking photos and we somehow got separated for a bit. When I finally caught up with him, I saw him just sitting there, peacefully, watching the sunset. And then, in that moment, I knew I needed to marry this man. I saw a thoroughly decent,

gorgeous man and knew I could love him for the rest of my life.'

- **Summary:** 'I suddenly knew, beyond reasonable doubt, that I couldn't live without him.'
- **Acknowledgement of the dearly departed (if necessary).**
- **Address your partner with a final romantic tribute.**
- **Toast:** 'I hereby sentence us both to a long and happy marriage. Please join me in a toast to . . . "beyond reasonable doubt".'

Say goodbye to content

Once you've nailed your theme, you'll spot that a lot of your content no longer works. Sorry about that.

Once you've gathered great content, letting it go can feel hard, but resist the urge to shoehorn everything in. The overall flow of the speech is more important than an individual story.

One idea to make use of some of your discarded content is to write a note to your partner to read on the morning of the wedding. It can be really simple and doesn't need to feel like an 'extra job'. For example . . .

'I can't wait to see you in a few hours' time.

'This morning, in amongst all the madness of getting ready, I just wanted to remind you about some of my favourite times with you . . .

'Do you remember when . . . (*Your personal stories*)?

'As we start the next chapter of our life together, I wanted to thank you for all the magical times we've shared so far. I'm already looking forward to creating many more with you as a married couple. See you at church!'

STEP 2 – STRUCTURE AND WRITE YOUR SPEECH

Okay, you've got the content and the big idea. Now it's time to write your speech and, seeing as we've got all our building blocks in place *and* a plan of action, this is going to be so much easier than looking at a blank screen would have been.

This stage is mostly about joining the dots.

It's also about understanding the parameters you're working within.

Speech length

'There's a great saying; delivering a speech shouldn't take longer than it does to consummate a marriage,' points out Alison Hargreaves.

Sticking with the innuendo: when it comes to speeches, size matters.

All the influencers and experts I spoke to said short is sweeter and listed long speeches as one of their pet hates. Several said they had heard marvellous speeches that lasted just a couple of minutes, while *all* of them said they had sat through a lengthy speech that bored them.

One of the main reasons I set up Speechy was because I had had a similar experience; a best man who went on for over forty minutes and refused to give up, even when heckled.

It really is foundation-level speechwriting. No one ever listened to a speech and said, 'I wish it was longer.'

A speech needs to be punchy, and increasingly so. Studies have shown that the global attention span is shrinking. Our desire for 'newness' and stimulation is growing.

Consequently, a twenty-minute speech rarely works. And I mean, *very* rarely. Maybe a Pulitzer Prize-winner could pull it off but, really, why would you want to give yourself that challenge?

The ideal length of a wedding speech is generally between 1,100 and 1,300 words.

To put this into perspective, Lincoln's Gettysburg Address was 272 words long.

Most speakers talk at about 150 words per minute. This means, allowing for laughter and ad libs, a 1,300-word speech will come in just less than ten minutes.

This might sound like a long time to some of you, but, trust us, it flies. You don't want to skimp on your speech or give yourself an unrealistic word count target.

I work with some couples who are convinced they want to deliver a *very* short speech ('two or three minutes max') and this poses as much of a challenge as a long speech. People who want short speeches generally have just as much to say as everyone else.

You *can* make a point with very few words, but I'd worry if your word count was lower than 750 if you're also thanking friends and family.

Structure

We've already looked at how themes work and given you an idea of a good speech structure, but to break it down further, the general rule is this . . .

- **Hello and welcome.**
- **The Speech-Meat** – Set-up of the theme, appropriate anecdotes, stories and insights. Summary of what the anecdotes and insights prove.
- **Thank-yous.**
- **Acknowledgement of the dearly departed (if necessary).**
- **Address your partner with a final romantic tribute.**
- **Toast.**

This structure may be different to most speeches you've heard. Many speakers automatically start with the thank-yous but, as important as they may be, they are *not* what really interests your guests.

You need to start strong, and that's with good storytelling. Kick off with the humour and end with the heartfelt. The emotional leap ensures the sentiment has more impact.

Don't script a thank-you to the previous speaker as the opening to your speech. Make this thank-you a spontaneous ad lib *before* you obviously start delivering your speech. This makes the thank-you sound like a genuine, heartfelt reaction rather than a 'tick-box' courtesy.

The cornerstones of your speech

YOUR OPENING

The opening of your speech might be one of the last things you write.

'We always find the start the hardest thing to do, so when we write, we start with the middle of the speech first,' say Ed Amsden and Tom Coles.

With all writing, you want to start and end with your strongest lines. At the beginning, you're winning your audience over, and at the end, you're leaving them thinking you're brilliant.

Many folk assume the first couple of sentences have to be a version of 'Good evening ladies and gentlemen. My partner and I . . . (*pause for applause*) would like to welcome you all here today and thank you for joining us to celebrate our marriage.'

Actually, that doesn't have to be the case. Sometimes it *can* be. But it shouldn't be automatic. Ask yourself if there's anything more exciting.

Don't waste people's time with the same dull wedding-waffle. Every word should count, so consider forgetting the 'hellos' altogether.

Controversial, I know.

The trick is to make the opening personal. Don't bother with the usual nonsense about what a lovely venue it is. Cut out the white noise. Cut to the punchline.

ALTERNATIVE OPENINGS

- **Jump right in.** 'So we've finally done it. Sophie has agreed to put up with me for the rest of her life and I've got that in writing.'
- **Address your audience.** 'Can I just say how lovely it is to be standing here, surrounded by our favourite people in the world – though I must admit, with us all suited and booted, I don't recognise half of you. I think this may be the first time (*the best man*) has been seen in public without a Ramones T-shirt on.'
- **Short and snappy.** If there has been a delay to the wedding – a swift 'Well, we're finally here ... just 242 days late.'
- **Start with a story.** 'Let me tell you a story ... when I first saw Tom, sitting in the bar, reading a book in the middle of the Saturday night chaos, I knew I had to speak to him. Only he was too absorbed in his John Grisham to notice me.'

You get the idea.

The point is, even if you do welcome your guests at the top, *think* about how you're doing it.

I see lots of people wasting five paragraphs, a full 45 seconds, with absolute guff. Talking about guests travelling far. What a special occasion it is. Pure cut-and-paste jobs.

You want to get off to a strong start for *your* sake as well as your audience. If you surprise and subvert expectations, it wakes the audience up and tells them they're in for a treat.

Humour works well and I'd recommend having some as soon as possible.

'I've given three best man speeches and each time it's been nerve-wracking. But it's true, the minute you get your first laugh, you can relax. People are immediately on your side. No one expects you to be a stand-up but they want you to do well and a bit of genuine humour works well. It relaxes people.'

TOM COLES

THE SPEECH-MEAT

You've got the plan, now it's just a case of writing it up. 'Just'.

If you find a keyboard intimidating, use a speech-to-text app and talk. Tell the stories you plan to use, out loud and in order, and see what the resulting transcript looks like.

It's easier to make something better than it is to stare at a blank screen.

Once you've got the bulk of your word count worked out, read through it and check you have touches of both humour and sentiment at regular points throughout the speech.

The type of language you use depends on you. Your speech should feel conversational; it doesn't need to be more poetic than your everyday language.

Swear words – depends on you but be considerate of *all* your guests. While the grans can probably handle the odd b-word, it may not be appropriate if there are children present. Innuendo is fine but being overtly crude isn't.

Ed Amsden and Tom Coles recommend, 'There are lines of taste you don't want to cross but if you're a sweary person, your guestlist probably already knows it. Use it for effect as opposed to casually.'

Your guests should be at the forefront of your mind throughout your writing process. If you're delivering your speech to an audience in a language that not everyone is fluent in, check with appropriate representatives to ensure that any expressions or proverbs you're using can still be easily understood.

As Alan Berg points out, 'Idioms never translate and even gestures have to be checked. A thumbs up is considered as rude as sticking up your middle finger in some cultures.'

He adds, 'Although it's sometimes effective to include colloquialisms from the other cultures present, do not attempt to mimic. If you're talking about the Irish love of "craic" or acknowledging the relatives from the Southern States with a "bless your heart", don't attempt any accents.'

THE TOAST

A good toast summarises the point of your speech. It's the ultimate call-back. It provides great storytelling symmetry and is a call to action for everyone present.

'It's basic journalism; the speech should start by telling me what you're going to tell me, you then tell the story and conclude by telling me what you've told me,' explains Andrew Shanahan.

For example, if you've adopted the modern fairy tale theme you could conclude it with:

'I may not be able to slay a dragon but I promise to make you laugh every day of your life.

'Can I ask you now to join me in a toast to a life filled with friends, family and fairy tales?

'To fairy tales.'

As Andrew says, 'The toast itself needs to be succinct enough to propose it and for people to second it. It's essentially a contract, so be concise.'

Specific styles of speeches

WRITE A JOINT SPEECH

As you know, I'm a huge fan of joint speeches but writing one does involve more effort than a solo number.

The same principles apply, however.

1 – Find your theme

Find that narrative hook that will hold everything together.

You can use the same theme suggestions that we covered on pages 118 to 125.

Let's say you both happen to be teachers, your theme might be the 'love lessons' classic.

Your structure might look something like this ...

- **Hello and welcome.**
- **Thank everyone for coming and set up the theme**, e.g. 'With two teachers getting married today ... you may be wondering who gets detention first.'

(*Point at each other*)

'Okay, we're not quite sure but what I can tell you is that we've learnt a lot from each other over the years. Some good, some bad ...'

- **Lesson 1** – What NOT to say on the first date:

Partner 1 explains how Partner 2 told a story about weeing themselves and almost getting arrested.

Partner 2 reveals how they were put off when Partner 1 confessed to loving *Below Deck* and admitted they had three maxed-out credit cards.

- **Lesson 2** – Love makes you do stupid things:

Partner 1 reveals Partner 2 booked a spontaneous holiday for them without checking if either of them had a valid passport. They didn't.

Partner 2 tells the story about how Partner 1 tried to impress the in-laws with a lemon cheesecake but used the pith of the lemon instead of the zest. (This may or may not be based on a true story. What can I say? I've never baked much.)

- **Lesson 3** – How to share a house with someone very different:

Partner 1 talks about the challenges of living with someone who thinks a ping-pong table is furniture.

Partner 2 talks about sharing a bed with someone who wakes up in the middle of the night screaming.

- **Lesson 4** – Why you choose to spend the rest of your life with someone:

Partner 1 shares their romantic stories and insights.
Partner 2 adds theirs.

Thank-yous.
Acknowledgement of the dearly departed (if necessary).
Toast.

2 – Split up

When it comes to writing the speech, this may or may not prove to be your toughest relationship challenge to date. You thought table planning was tricky? It's nothing compared to writing a joint speech. My advice? Avoid it!

Yes, one of you write the first draft and the other one improve it. Even this will require some negotiation but at least you won't be debating words as you write.

Divide the speech so you each have small sections to deliver (2–6 sentences) and alternate throughout. You want to support each other's narrative. For example . . .

Groom: It was a surprise finding out we were going to have a baby. Neither of us had changed a nappy in our lives and we didn't have a clue. We'd never watched a minute of Nickelodeon let alone three hours of it back-to-back.

Bride: We couldn't have imagined a time when being up at two in the morning didn't involve drinking beer and passing out under someone's table.

Groom: And we could never have imagined the tantrums that could result from feeding a toddler with the wrong-coloured spoon.

Bride: But the one thing that we had absolutely no idea about was how amazing having a child would be.

Like all good comedy duos, you need to work together. Script your comedy 'ad libs'. If your relationship dynamic lends itself, one of you can play the straight man and the other the fall guy. Play with what you got.

3 – Length
Just because there's two of you, doesn't mean the speech can be double the length. In fact, you're really only allowed an extra couple of hundred words, so 1,450 maximum.

4 – Rehearse
The good news is the sole pressure of delivering your speech is off. The bad news? Delivering your speech has become a bit more complicated.

Yes, the ease of a double act takes some rehearsal. Especially if you want the 'ad libs' to look natural.

So, practise your interaction. Smile, roll your eyes, look at one another and play off each other.

Eduardo Braniff adds, 'Your delivery needs to reflect your genuine relationship dynamic. So if one of you is always talking over the other, reflect that.

'You also need to think about what you're doing when the other person is talking. Make sure you look at the person talking and react. Don't just lose yourself in your notes!'

WRITE A RHYMING SPEECH
Delivering a rhyming speech can make you seem cleverer than you actually are. It's also an easy way to come across as a pre-schooler reading a poem about their teddy.

It just depends on your ability. Even if you get the rhyming spot on, you also have to nail the rhythm (a much harder thing to do).

It is a RISK. But if you do decide to go for it, here's the cheat's guide to writing a poem.

- Decide what point you're trying to make with the speech and the stories you're wanting to tell. Pull out all the keywords from that content; the ones that are crucial to telling the story and the punchline words.
- Use a thesaurus to find as many variations of those keywords as possible.
- Next, use a rhyming dictionary to come up with words that rhyme with the keywords and their variants.
- Spot the rhyming words that could fit into the theme of your speech. Pull out all the useful pairs of words (a keyword and a rhyming word).
- Now, build your poem using your pairings to create rhyming sentences.
- Sometimes it's easier to find a poem that you like to base your rhythm on. For example, use a Pam Ayres poem and base your effort on a similar beat.
- Put the more tenuous rhyming word or sentence first. The second 'payoff' sentence is the one that your poetry is judged on. This is also where the punchline should be.
- Once you write your first verse, ensure that all the others follow the same pattern and rhythm.
- One comedy technique is to set up the idea that you're about to say something rude, but after a pause, reveal something completely innocent. For example, my sister-in- law included this classic in her sister-of-the-groom speech . . . 'He erected a tent, thought that should do the trick, then he took her to a nudist beach to show off his . . . suntan.'

STEP 3 – EDIT YOUR SPEECH

Ernest Hemingway is quoted as saying 'The first draft of anything is shit.' And that's someone who won the Nobel Prize for Literature.

Your first draft is just the *start* of the writing process.

As Andrew Shanahan says, 'Once it's written, leave it for a weekend. You'll come back to it and might think it's better than you remember. Or, of course, worse.'

Word count edit

The first thing to look at is the length. Even if it's under 1,300 words, it will, I promise, be made better by reducing your word count.

Alan Berg points out: 'There's the expression, "If I had more time, I would have written a shorter letter."' The quote is thought to have derived from the writing legend Mark Twain and it goes to show how hard the editing process can be.

With Speechy's Edit Service, the main thing we do is make the speech punchier. We look at the overall structure and see if all the stories and lines are actually necessary. Do they really add much?

We then look at every sentence and see if every word is needed. Generally, the shorter the sentence, the more impact it will have.

As Eduardo Braniff says, 'The fastest and tightest speeches are the best. To quote Coco Chanel, "Before you leave the house, look in the mirror and take one thing off." Make every sentence matter.'

Test the theory out. Save your first draft but then get busy with that delete function. Cut your word count by a third. Do you lose much?

As Kat Williams notes, 'We have a tendency to over-explain things. We think people need to know all the detail but they don't.'

The editing process can feel brutal but it's vital. It might mean you have to drop some of your favourite lines but no one will miss them. Your guests didn't know they existed.

The audio edit

It's now time to start reading your speech out loud.

We don't speak in the same form as we write, the sentence construction is different, so does your speech feel overly formal? Are there sections or words that you keep tripping over? Does the punchline need to be moved?

Alan Berg says, 'Your mind doesn't get tongue-tied, your tongue does, so reading your speech out loud is essential in perfecting your speech.'

Stage 3 recap

- Find your theme, either by selecting your best stories and finding a thread that links them, or by thinking about the point you want to make and *then* finding the stories.
- Make sure your speech is less than 1,300 words.
- Don't open with wedding-waffle. Start strong.
- Can you make your toast original?
- Joint speeches are great but are more challenging to write.
- Attempting a rhyming speech is tricky to pull off.
- A brutal edit will improve any speech.

SPEECH INSPIRATION

Groom speech – Delivered by Alejandro

Background: Alejandro has married Michelle. They live in Boston. Alejandro is in his fifties and is originally from Spain. There are lots of people at the wedding for whom English is their second language.

Ladies and gentlemen, friends and family, Spaniards and Americans – today is an historic day. As Michelle has done me the great honour of agreeing to be my wife, it is a day when our countries' traditions and cultures come together.

Today, the Spanish Imperial Eagle takes to the skies with the American Bald Eagle. Today, we scatter hamburgers and fries across the paella and create the McPaella. Today, we play the Marcha Real alongside the Star-Spangled Banner.

(*Music mash-up of the two national anthems played at the same time*)

As you can perhaps tell, a mix of cultures is not always an easy thing, but I believe that, with work, my wife and I can make it so that our music is harmonious, our meals are delicious and our nations' birds do not peck each other to death.

Today, I have the joy of standing here as part of a married couple. As you may know, I am more mature than the traditional groom and I must admit that as, one-by-one, my friends and family members all got married, I sat there at a succession of weddings, always on the single table. In case you were wondering, the single table is Table Five today. Please stop by and pity them, it's what they deserve.

At every wedding I was pestered by my mother and aunts about when I will marry. I looked at the grooms and I thought, 'Thank God I am single.' I will admit I have enjoyed the bachelor life. I have enjoyed being free to pursue my work, to not worry about when I come home, and to live in a house where there are fewer than two cushions in the entire place.

But then Michelle happened.

We met through the intervention of our friend Katya – there she is on Table Five, and, yes, she is single. I met Michelle in the street as we were passing and she was rude to me and bossy. I couldn't understand this American powerhouse. She told me to take her out for coffee and I don't know what happened. I lost the power to resist. All of my bachelor strength was drained, and I found myself nodding and doing as I was told for once.

I don't know how but Michelle flies under my radar, she unpicks my defences and I find it impossible to resist her. And I have tried!

So, my beautiful wife Michelle arrived and my bachelor life ended. I am able to stand here today and say I am so grateful that it has. No more Table Five. No more aunts and mothers asking me when I will get married. So many more cushions.

Michelle has allowed me to speak for both of us today, which she did on the condition that I understood this was to be the last time in our married lives that this was the case. From now on, I shall be the perfect trophy husband that Michelle wants, I will nod and I will look pretty.

I would like to take this opportunity then to say some sincere and heartfelt thank-yous. First of all, I would like to thank you, our guests, for coming today. I know that for some of you, especially the guests today from Malaga in southern Spain, the journey to join us here today has been significant.

When people will fly nearly 5,000 miles to a wedding, you realise how powerful the offer of free food and drink truly is. I hope today is a celebration for you too and please know that we are so grateful for you making this day so special.

Now for the rest of you, I want to issue a warning that many of our Malagan guests might not have the greatest command of the English language. For some of them this is the first time that they have been abroad. I won't embarrass him by name, but one of the guests asked me where Mickey Mouse was and I had to explain that the mouse isn't everywhere.

So, to make them feel more welcome I thought maybe I could teach you some useful Spanish phrases that could help you integrate. If you look on your table you will see a card for you each so you can read along with me. So listen to me and repeat please!

'He bebido demasiado Sangria y no puedo sentir mis piernas.'

Come on, I know you can do it.

'He bebido demasiado Sangria y no puedo sentir mis piernas.'

That is a very useful Spanish phrase which means:

'I have drunk too much Sangria and can no longer feel my legs.'

Okay, another:

'Me gustaria bailar Flamenco contigo hasta una hora desaconsejable.'

Try again:

'Me gustaria bailar Flamenco contigo hasta una hora desaconsejable.'

That means:

'I would like to dance the flamenco with you until an inadvisable hour.'

Excellent! Now finally:

'Hola, me puedes llamar un Uber. No recuerdo nada de anoche.'

Again:

'Hola, me puedes llamar un Uber. No recuerdo nada de anoche.'

That translates as:

'Please call me an Uber, I have no recollection of last night.'

Now, as you may know I have been in America for nearly ten years now and I am starting to think of myself as part-American. For Michelle, I know this makes her laugh, because she often says that I am the most Spanish man in the history of the world.

But I think coming to a foreign country can be an amazing learning experience because every day you do things as an outsider. Everything is different here. Everything. You want to go to the toilet in America then you have to pay to go into the toilet. In America, toilets are also a business! Amazing!

I am an outsider with your food. Thanks to my mother I was raised eating home-cooked food bursting with flavour, then I come to America and I eat McDonald's every day and slowly my tastebuds fade away and now they are on life support, kept going only by the *jamon iberico* my mother sends me at Christmas.

But as an outsider I have also been shocked to see the

difference in some people in America – the friendliness and the warmth that I am offered. I think this is why Michelle has overcome my defences.

As you know, she works as the director of a charity and she lives her life for other people. She thinks and she cares for other people all the time and I am amazed that she has agreed to be my wife today. Perhaps I am her biggest charity project yet and one day after years of rehabilitation she will release me back into the wild. I hope not.

By contrast, I am the greedy property developer, making money from the ruins of other people's lives and hopes. I will not lie, my day is not complete until I have pushed at least three widows out of their houses and turned their homes into flats. But maybe this too has been useful for my marriage. After all, my work has taught me to look at ruined and dilapidated things and see the beauty there. Anyone drawing any comparisons to Michelle should be ashamed of themselves.

Seriously, I couldn't imagine a more beautiful woman on any continent in the world today.

I want to thank you for coming to our wedding. I want to thank Michelle for agreeing to be my wife and I want to end my speech by offering her these traditional *arras*. These are Spanish gold coins that a groom gives to his wife on their wedding day. The coins are a symbol of how the man promises to provide for his wife. Not just in terms of finance but also for their emotions – to be a provider that gives her everything she needs.

My love, I give these coins to you today and promise that I will do my best to ensure that for the rest of our lives you have everything you ever need and, always, more than enough love.

Now everybody: please raise your glasses and repeat after me: '¡Arriba! ¡Abajo! ¡Al centro! . . . y pa dentro!' That means put your arm up, put your arm down, health for you all, drink it down!

SPEECH WRITTEN BY ANDREW SHANAHAN

GUS: Good evening, ladies and gentlemen.

PAOLO: Although having been clubbing with many of you back in the day, I'm not sure 'gentlemen' is the right term. Now, as many of you know, my new husband Gus isn't the most confident in a big crowd, which is why I'll be doing most of the talking today.

GUS: And I'll be saying the occasional word, but mainly nodding in agreement.

PAOLO: Just think of it like one of our dinner parties. Only with much, *much* better catering.

GUS: For our speech today, we wanted to do something a little different, and rather than give a speech, we thought we'd tell you a story.

PAOLO/GUS: A rather unusual fairy tale.

PAOLO: Now, a long, long time ago, in a land far, far away …

GUS: Ruislip.

PAOLO: … there was a frog. Now, this frog was half-Italian, had *slightly* greying hair, and was allergic to the gym. Honestly, it was like a fairy tale curse! If he even touched a weights bench, he'd die instantly.

GUS: Always good to have an excuse.

PAOLO: This frog wasn't brought up by a wicked stepmother or an evil snow queen, but by his dad, Frank, who was a long-haul lorry driver. Yes, it was less 'Snow White and the 7 Dwarves', and more 'White americano on the M7 motorway'.

GUS: As a teenager, the frog dreamt of meeting his prince. But little did the little Italian frog know that his true love was lurking around the corner.

PAOLO: In Guildford. We told you this was an *unconventional* fairy tale, right? This young Prince Charming was, like all princes, a pampered little lad, enrolled in a private school and engaging in the most expensive hobbies.

GUS: Horse-riding, sailing, even violin lessons.

PAOLO: Whereas my hobbies *made* me money. If you count stealing tenners from my dad's wallet as a hobby, that is. And though they were from two different worlds, the frog and the prince would eventually meet, many years later, in the court of love.

GUS:	Or as most people refer to it: PlentyOfFish.com.
PAOLO:	Yes, for our two heroes it had been many years of being unlucky in love, with failed relationships, awkward dates and even three months with a woman called Julie . . . Let's just say it didn't take long to realise we should just be friends. But now, the prince and the frog were united.
GUS:	All they needed now was the kiss. For their first kiss, they needed somewhere beautiful, romantic, straight out of a magical storybook.
PAOLO:	That's right, ladies and gents: outside Tiger Tiger nightclub in Croydon.
GUS:	But still, the kiss was wonderful and the spell was broken. And Paolo was no longer a poor, lonely frog.
PAOLO:	Now he was a 42-year-old frog snogging posh blokes outside a nightclub. He'd truly come such a long way.
GUS:	Soon, the pair were in love, and moved into their very own castle.
PAOLO:	And yes, instead of a moat, there was damp on the ceiling.

GUS:	Instead of a drawbridge, there was a sign saying, 'doorbell broken, please shout'.
PAOLO:	And instead of a palace jester, there was Maureen the landlord with her insistence on calling us 'the two friends in Flat B'.
GUS:	But it's a castle to us, and we couldn't love it more.
PAOLO:	Finally, all that was left was the fairy tale wedding. Esteemed, noble guests gathered from far and wide, a devilish feast was eaten, and one thousand bottles of wine were drunk.
GUS:	And that was just my sister, Becca.
PAOLO:	Deciding to get married was the prince's most expensive hobby yet – who knew it would cost a thousand pounds to hire chairs?!
GUS:	If I ever get married again, you lot can sit on the floor like a primary school assembly.
PAOLO:	But despite the cost, the wedding was beautiful. Merry minstrels played melodic music, and heartfelt vows were shared.
GUS:	Which means I've had to speak in public twice today.

PAOLO:	And from that moment on, the frog and the prince lived happily ever after. A bigger, less damp castle is on the horizon, and hopefully even some little half-prince, half-frog babies.
GUS:	Although when you put it like that, it's a little off-putting.
PAOLO:	So, as this storybook comes to an end, a new one begins. Please join us in raising a toast, to the next chapter.
PAOLO/GUS:	*(raise glasses)* The next chapter!
PAOLO:	Before we leave you, we did want to give a nod to those who sadly couldn't be with us today. Frank the lorry driver was a huge fan of Gus, and he would have been over the moon to see us tie the knot today. And I hope I made my mother Shirley proud as well.
GUS:	I never got to meet Shirley, but from everything I've heard, she is the one who gave Paolo his kindness, his sense of community, and his absolutely terrible dress sense. For those of you we were able to welcome today, special thanks must go to my parents, Val and Jim, for all their love and support, and of course to the aforementioned Becca. How's that Chablis going down, sis?
PAOLO:	To our Best – and I use that term inaccurately – Men, Liam and Joe, thanks for all your help today, and of course a huge

thanks to Steffi for being a logistical queen. We couldn't have done it without you.

GUS: It isn't easy planning a wedding for a pampered prince with very expensive tastes ...

PAOLO: Or a greying frog who never shuts up ...

GUS: But you did it. Thank you.

PAOLO: Right, that's all from us, other than to borrow a quote from Hans Christian Andersen: 'Life itself is the most wonderful fairy tale.'

GUS: And to borrow a quote from Frank the lorry driver: 'Alright buddy, fancy a pint?'

SPEECH WRITTEN BY ED AMSDEN AND TOM COLES

Well, hello everyone! Seeing as Xavier has already had two goes at doing a wedding speech, I thought maybe this time, I'd have a turn. Third time isn't lucky in all things.

I honestly never, in all my days, thought I would be standing here doing a speech at my own wedding. Especially not at my age. I truly believed the first time I walked down the aisle would be the only time. Because back then I was twenty-one, and so obviously I knew everything.

By the time I met Xavier twenty-five years later, I had discovered I, of course, knew absolutely nothing. In fact, the only thing I *did* know about love was, I wanted nothing at all to do with it!

I had my family, my two gorgeous children, Milly and Lance, I had a wonderful group of girlfriends, and I had my dogs. Who needed anything more?

Well, it turned out, life had a few more lessons for me yet.

To be honest, I was slightly annoyed when I turned up at Milly's graduation to realise she was clearly trying to set me up with her friend Samuel's father. Oh, he was handsome alright. Too handsome if you asked me. I knew *all* about handsome men. They were to be avoided at all costs!

But, when the kids went off to collect their diplomas, I learnt something fascinating about this tall, dark, handsome stranger. He had absolutely no interest in love either. Divorced twice, he was as happy to settle down with his dogs as I was.

So, together, we hatched a plan. At the meal the kids had organised that evening, we would flirt so wildly with one another, they would be horrified, and never set us up with anyone ever again. Well, this was a plan I could get on board with. I said I wasn't interested in falling in love, I never said I wasn't interested in flirting with a handsome stranger. I was a 54-year-old mother, not a nun!

As we had guessed, the kids were mortified. We laughed, we played with each other's hair, we made some *very* smutty jokes. I'm not sure I've ever had more fun. By the time the dessert menu came round, the kids couldn't wait to get us out of there.

Once we were back at our hotel room, I told Milly what had really happened, and I couldn't tell if she was more furious, or relieved. I was surprised the next day when he added me on Facebook, but I didn't think too much about it.

But love lesson number one was: sometimes even fake flirting can do the job.

Every time one of Xavier's posts came up on my newsfeed, I couldn't help but smile, remembering that night. How nice it had been to have a handsome man tell me my 'eyes sparkled like the stars on Midsummer's Eve'. Even if he hadn't meant a word of it.

My friends started rolling their eyes whenever I began retelling the story for the 114th time. Or mentioned Xavier's name in passing. But I knew it was nothing. Just my last flirtation before I slipped into old lady hibernation. I had my cardigans ready and everything.

So when I saw Xavier's beloved dog had sadly passed away, I thought nothing of sending him a little message of condolence, just as a friend. And I thought nothing of him sending me a little thank-you note back. Which, of course, it was only polite to respond to.

Which is when I learnt love lesson number two.

A single woman really can't just be friends with a very handsome single man.

Soon we were messaging every day. Which was ridiculous because I absolutely knew he wasn't interested. And neither was

I. So it was harmless for us to meet for a few drinks, right? And the kids didn't even have to know!

So I was surprised, and more than a little delighted, that when we finally met after three months of messaging he was just as charming and flirtatious as he'd been that very first time. We laughed and we talked and we smiled until my cheeks hurt. Which is when I learnt love lesson number three.

You're never too old to be giddy as a schoolgirl.

Of course, love lesson number four came hot on its heels.

The course of true love never runs smoothly.

Being an old-fashioned broad, it never crossed my mind that my gorgeous, charming, flirtatious Latin lover could be dating other women. So when Milly casually mentioned on the phone that she and Samuel had bumped into Xavier on a date the night before ... and I knew I'd been at home all night watching re-runs of *Grey's Anatomy* ... well ...

Let's just say, if the government really are monitoring our Facebook messages, then someone saw some very choice words that day!

But after *a lot* of grovelling, Xavier explained that he hadn't thought we were exclusive. After all, hadn't I told him over and over that I wasn't interested in love? It was then I learnt love lesson number five.

Honesty is the best policy. Particularly when it came to being honest with myself.

I really wasn't ready to hang up my heart just yet. I wanted to be with Xav. And so, we finally made things official.

Although we did have to blur the lines on that honesty policy a little. Turns out, if I ask Xavier if my outfit looks nice *just* as I'm leaving the house, sometimes a little white lie helps move things along. Same goes for me and my critique of his cooking.

And along the way, we've learnt some other little love lessons too. That no matter how much you adore a person, their snoring can lead to some very vivid murder fantasies. That sometimes it's easier to just hire a cleaner. And I've learnt that Manchester United is the most superior football club in the world, and I must never say anything else, even if I don't follow football at all.

But I've also learnt that opening up my heart again has been the most wonderful, delicious and exhilarating thing I could ever do. Xavier, you have brought so much love and light into my life. Knowing you will be waiting for me at home when I'm having a stressful day makes everything that little bit easier.

You've brought adventure to this old gal's life, taking me to Cuba and Thailand and Bali, showing me all kinds of amazing sights – not least the sight of you in those tiny swimming shorts you wear.

And yes, between us, we have far too many dogs, and even the amount of children and grandchildren is starting to get out of hand. But I love every single bit of it. Before I met you, I truly believed I had more than enough love in my life. You have shown me that my heart is limitless.

And I know now that you can be wholly and completely in love at any age. And I'll never be too old to learn more, and to love more.

I'm so excited to watch you grow even greyer, to welcome even more dogs and grandchildren, and for my heart to grow even bigger. Thank you for taking another chance on love, and for becoming my husband.

If you could all please be upstanding for the toast.

To life's lessons.

SPEECH WRITTEN BY CLAIRE WETTON

Stage 4 – Deliver Your Speech

Strong delivery is just as important as a brilliant speech.

A great speech can lose all its charm, humour and power by a rushed delivery, a nervous demeanour or, worse still, if people can't actually hear it.

Good delivery takes natural confidence and charisma or, for the 95 per cent of us who don't come equipped with that, a hell of a lot of practice and knowing some basic delivery techniques.

I picked up the presenting principles when I was working in TV, directing both professional presenters and members of the public. It was my job to get the best out of people and, although everyone's style is different, I discovered there are a few essential pieces of advice that can help nearly *everyone* present better.

The plan

This stage comes in four parts:

1 **Preparing to deliver:** deciding whether you should use notes, memorisation techniques, and what makes a strong delivery.
2 **Delivery goals and presenting principles.**
3 **Handling nerves:** how to become more confident.
4 **Delivery on the day:** your pre-speech, mid-speech and post-speech checklists (yes, you read correctly, a *post*-speech reminder!).

EXPERT INSIGHT

'Okay, when writing your wedding speech, I said approach it like a business speech but delivering a wedding speech is NOT like a business speech. A wedding is actually a very alien environment and it's natural to feel a bit intimidated.

'Make good eye contact and smile! Good vibes create good vibes.'

ANNA PRICE OLSON

'Most people underestimate the power of a pause. Far too many speeches are rushed; you have to give the line a moment to sink in. It adds weight to it.'

EDUARDO BRANIFF

'Remember, you don't need to be perfect. You're in front of friends, not a court hearing. And sometimes the imperfections are what make a speech memorable.'

KAT WILLIAMS

'My number one piece of advice would always be to time your drinks! You don't want to hear your name called and realise you've had one too many to read your cue cards.

'Something else I always notice in a great speech is eye contact. Try to consciously address the person you're speaking to or about.'

HAMISH SHEPHARD

'Beware going off script on the day. The dreaded Biden effect; where you've got a great speech scripted and then you get carried away and add an ad lib that ruins the whole thing.'

ALISON HARGREAVES

'When I'm preparing for a speech, I record myself and listen to it repeatedly. In the car, at home, wherever. I then try to improve it, record that next version and then listen to that repeatedly.

'I keep repeating the process until the speech becomes this song, a melody that's ingrained in me. Given enough time, delivering your speech can feel like singing along to your favourite song.'

ALAN BERG

PREPARE TO DELIVER

Take note

The first thing to think about is if and how you'll use notes.

As Andrew Shanahan points out, 'Delivering without notes is like doing a wheelie; pretty cool but, ultimately, unnecessary. It's just showing off really.'

Yes, there's a joy in witnessing someone's spontaneous thinking (even if that 'spontaneity' has been scripted and memorised), but unless you are very experienced at public speaking, going freestyle isn't for the fainthearted.

And, even if you *are* a highly capable speaker in a business context, a wedding audience is unlike any other you've presented to, so I would *still* recommend having notes to hand.

Notes are not a sign of weakness, it's simply evidence that you've prepared. And why, if you've spent weeks perfecting your speech, would you just aim to deliver a sloppy version of it?

Alan Berg says, 'I'm never impressed by a waitress who doesn't write the order down. Write it down. Get it right.'

HOW TO PRESENT YOUR NOTES

Paper, cue cards or tech?

It comes down to personal preference but my recommendation, every time, is old-school A4 paper.

Mobiles and iPads are increasingly being used and they will inevitably become more prevalent, but, personally, I'm not convinced. Tech may be what you expect a modern couple to use but I think it looks overly casual and sends out the wrong message.

How many of us get annoyed when our loved ones get lost looking at a screen? For many of us, feeling frustrated is an inherent reaction when someone looks at their phone in our company.

Devices are excluding and they imply you're in another world. And, although many people assume a device is easier to handle than pieces of paper, in my experience it's clumsier. You end up scrolling too far or accidentally flicking on to another page. So, personally, I wouldn't risk it.

I suspect I'll always prefer cue cards and paper. And paper trumps. Less flicking necessary.

I advise buying good quality paper that's slightly thicker than your standard office A4. Ideally something between 120 and 140gsm to help reduce paper-shake.

HOW TO LAY OUT YOUR SPEECH
Bullet points or word for word?

Some people use bullet points so their speech comes across as more natural and they can focus on establishing good eye contact with their audience.

A good idea in principle but test it out.

Are you good enough to deliver all those wonderful anecdotes and insights in an eloquent way whilst also remembering that punchline and where exactly it goes? Do you wander off track and add unnecessary waffle? Crucially, are you delivering the speech in a way that sounds *genuinely* natural, or is it obvious that you're struggling to remember your lines?

The danger of using bullet points is, instead of looking like you're reading your speech, it looks like you're trying to *remember* your speech; delivering it like a terrified bunny, eyes wide, devoid of the actual emotion intended.

So, I recommend that you print out your speech word-for-word.

- Lay it out on A4 so that **the bottom third of the page has no text.** This means your eyeline doesn't drop too low.
- **Ensure the page turn is at an appropriate point** i.e. after a story has concluded, where you'd expect laughter or if there's a natural pause.
- **Codify your speech.** Use bold or italics to help you remember emphasis. Use ellipses (the three dots) to pinpoint where you should pause. Add regular reminders (even just a coloured asterisk) throughout the speech to ensure you are still smiling (honestly, people often need reminding).
- **Use a symbol.** Ampersands (&) work well as a reminder to add an 'ad lib' – i.e. a line that you've scripted but memorised so you deliver it 'off script'. This is a great technique that ensures you seem spontaneously witty and more relaxed than you may feel.
- **Use page numbers.** In case you drop the speech.

Memorise your speech

Having notes is no excuse to be lazy.

While I encourage clients to use notes, I also stress the importance of memorising the speech or, at least, ensuring the words are deep-rooted. You need to be familiar with the flow of it.

On the day, you should only be using your notes to *reference*, rather than read from. It's something you should be glancing at, not reading.

Rehearse as often as you can. Memorising something is *meant* to be hard. No one enjoys doing it but the more you put into it, the easier it will get.

Memorise your speech until it bores you. In the weeks leading up to the wedding, surround yourself with it. As Alan Berg suggests, record yourself reading it and listen to it repeatedly. On your commute, going to bed, whenever you can.

Studies have suggested a few extra techniques *might* help retention...

- Write out the speech by hand (typing doesn't count).
- Read the speech out loud three times in succession.
- Recite the speech just before you go to bed.
- Try delivering the speech without notes. If you lose track, pick up where you left off and force yourself to carry on.

But, really, there's no big secret to memorisation.

It's just a case of speech, sleep, repeat.

DELIVERY GOALS

The aim is to come across as eloquent, confident and conversational. You also want to look like you're having fun.

Every client I work with has different delivery challenges to overcome (nerves being the only constant) but having watched presenters at work for over a decade, I've identified a few key factors in delivering your speech like a pro.

The presenting principles

PROSODY

This is the linguistic area concerned with intonation, stress and the rhythm of your speaking. It's what adds life to your speech. It can change an average sentence into something magical.

As a Scot, I have a head start. I have a naturally lilty, expressive sing-song to my voice. If you know you're prone to a monotone style (and so many people are) then work at reprogramming your brain.

Record your speech and consider where emphasis should be.

Experiment with the undulations of your delivery. It will feel odd initially; like you're hamming it up, but you need to do a bit of that. You need to *act* out your speech, not simply deliver it.

If you have a flat style of speaking, pretend you're telling a story to a toddler. Get expressive. Become playful.

Once you've nailed it, codify your speech accordingly (see page 157).

PACE

For years, the Speechy website was advising speakers to slow down; that a more deliberate pace helps people sound more assured. And for *some* people, that is the case.

Talking too fast is a big problem and I've heard too many speeches where it's obvious that the speaker just wants to get through it and sit down again. Rushing your delivery makes guests feel uncomfortable and creates a nervous atmosphere for everyone.

However, once I started providing delivery coaching, I realised not everyone was challenged in the same way. Turns out some people already talk at a leisurely pace and slowing them down made their style seem robotic.

So, how do you strike the balance between authority and confidence, and sounding like you're playing a podcast at half speed?

Well, what you're aiming for is a conversational tone. You want the pace of a chat with your friends, anywhere between 130 and 170 words per minute.

Time yourself and check your pace.

PLAN TO PAUSE

A conversational style includes pauses.

A pause is essential when you expect laughter, and you should never talk over it once it lands. Speakers often move on from the joke too quickly and don't give their audience a chance to react.

When I delivered my wedding speech, I didn't want it to come across as if I was lapping up the laughter so I gave my guests just a few seconds before launching into the rest of the speech. What a shame. Not only was I cutting short a great moment, I also ensured that my friends and family missed the first half of what I was continuing to say.

So, practise your pauses. And remember, they can be used to underline a sentimental thought too.

After each thank-you, take a second to make eye contact and nod your head towards the person you're addressing. After delivering a romantic line, take the time to look at your partner and smile. These moments can feel just as meaningful as the words themselves.

BODY LANGUAGE

It's a biggie. As well as *sounding* relaxed, you need to *look* relaxed. An audience picks up body language cues.

You may have heard of the 'power pose' that Amy Cuddy brought to the world via her TED Talk in 2012. Can standing in a 'powerful' and expansive way *really* make you feel more assertive? Well, subsequent studies suggest not, but hey, the basic idea makes sense . . . 'fake it till you make it.'

Film yourself and check your posture.

- Are your shoulders back?
- Do you look relaxed?
- Is your chin upwards and your head tilted towards your guests?
- Are you using your hands?
- Are you using facial expressions to full effect? Facial expressions can add an extra layer of humour so work on this. I want at least a couple of eyebrow raises in there.

- Are you smiling? Other than for any dearly departeds, I hope you are smiling throughout.

THE IMPORTANCE OF SMILING

This deserves a bit of emphasis.

Smiling has been scientifically proven to be infectious. A smile puts your guests at ease and it will help relax you too.

Even a *fake* smile has a beneficial effect on your body. Yes, researchers have shown even a phoney smile makes you feel happier.

And, a minute into your speech, that fake smile will become real.

EYE CONTACT

Eye contact increases trust and connection, so rehearse this too. Imagine who you're specifically addressing throughout the speech.

Crucially, look at your partner when you're talking to them. Allow this moment to breathe for added effect.

TROUBLESHOOTING

Vocal fillers

I'm guilty of this, using 'er' far too often.

It's something linguists call the hesitation phenomenon. You use filler words to allow your speech to catch up with your train of thought. It makes people think you're nervous and it's a hard habit to break.

So what can you do?

- **Slow down** – It's hard to catch up with your train of thought if you talk fast.

- **Plan the pause** – Plan strategic pauses throughout your speech to add drama, humour and poignancy. When you have planned pauses, you are less likely to have spontaneous ones that you feel you need to fill.
- **Rehearse** – The more comfortable you are with the flow of the speech, the calmer your mind will be.

Feedback

Employ a trusted friend (or your partner) and make the rehearsal as realistic as possible.

Start by sitting, get them to introduce you and, if you'll be using a microphone and notes on the day, make sure you're using both in the rehearsal too (even if the mic is a hairbrush).

After they've given their feedback, push for more; at least one piece of constructive criticism.

Ask specifics to make the feedback as useful as possible . . .

- Did I make enough eye contact?
- How was my pace?
- Were there any sections that lost you?
- Did your attention dip at any point?
- Did I smile enough?
- How was my body language?

And here's the crucial bit: once you receive their feedback, act on it. If they say they didn't get your favourite line, work out why and change it.

And, when it comes to feedback, Alan Berg suggests you go one step further: 'If you really want to push yourself, rehearse in front of strangers!'

HANDLING NERVES

The thought of speaking to a crowd of people you care about can be more terrifying than presenting to a room of work colleagues. But why?

Well, it can feel a bit judge-y can't it? Sure, you know everyone in the room is there to support you but they're also going to have an opinion about your speech.

When it comes to wedding planning, no one is going to blame you if the cake tastes a bit 'meh' or the DJ plays 'I Will Survive' but you *are* responsible for the speech you're delivering, and being the focus of everyone's attention, even for less than ten minutes, can be overwhelming.

When I work with clients on their delivery, *all* of them confess to being nervous, but the first thing I tell them is . . .

1 – THIS IS NOT ABOUT YOU

I get it. I used to get really nervous whenever I did public speaking. I was concentrating so hard on presenting, I forgot to breathe. And it turns out breathing is kind of important.

The only thing that worked for me was taking the emphasis off *me* delivering a great speech and instead, viewing it as me delivering a speech that's *great*.

I put the emphasis on the content, rather than me.

If you know you have a good speech on your hands, focus on conveying the humour and the sentiment to your audience. Imagine you're reading a story to pre-schoolers again. Drop all your pretensions and, instead, engross yourself in the story: the silly voices, the exaggerated facial expressions, the works.

See yourself as a conduit, a messenger of a story that is more important and more interesting than you. Don't think about yourself but how you can get the best possible reaction from your audience.

And remember, this isn't a business presentation where you'll be grilled on your PowerPoint statistics afterwards. Logically, you have nothing to worry about. So what if you fluff a line? Does it really matter if you lose your place?

Ultimately, there are *no* negative consequences to you messing this up. Your partner has already married you.

2 – ACCEPT THE NERVES

'Even the most experienced speakers get nervous,' says Alison Hargreaves.

You're not alone in feeling anxious. In fact, it would be odd if you weren't.

So prepare to be nervous.

Many professional public speakers have routines they employ prior to getting on stage to get them 'in the zone'. Some use breathing techniques (deep, slow breaths which you can do in your seat prior to standing up), others use more active exercises.

The motivational coach Tony Robbins does both. Meditation, breathing techniques and a full-on body workout with push-ups, press-ups and, often, a trampoline involved too.

Supposedly, it wakes both his mind and his body and energises his performance. Sounds exhausting to me, but watching his performances suggests it works.

Of course, it's unlikely you'll want to get sweaty just before delivering your speech or find an opportunity to do a full-body workout, but maybe a few squat jumps outside the marquee might work for you.

Test out your strategy in advance.

3 – ACKNOWLEDGE YOUR NERVES

You should never start your speech by saying you're nervous. As Alan Berg says, 'It's as if you're apologising for your speech before it's even started. You're immediately discrediting the speech that's about to come.'

However, I think it's good to have a couple of lines in your back pocket should you really stumble or feel you need them. Admitting to your audience that you're nervous can take the edge off.

'Dudes, I'm a little nervous. To be fair, I've just got married, I'm wearing a tight suit and I haven't had even a glass of champagne yet, so forgive me if I stumble over some words in my rush to get to the bar.'

Or something like, 'Gosh, I'm surprisingly nervous here, maybe because I know there are professional hecklers in the audience' can also take the focus off you for a second.

4 – TRICK YOURSELF
Breathe deeply and smile. Fool your body into thinking you're feeling more relaxed than you are.

ON-THE-DAY DELIVERY CHECKLISTS

Pre-delivery checklist

- **Have a snack** – An empty stomach isn't good for nerves. It may be the last thing you fancy but stuff a handful of canapés down or have a Mars bar on hand.
- **Don't drink alcohol** – Dutch courage is a myth. Alcohol actually *increases* stress levels.
- **Drink water** – A glass of water a few minutes prior to speaking will ensure you don't dry up.
- **Look for friendly faces in the audience** – And at different points of the room.

On-the-mic checklist

- **Stand up, breathe deep and smile.**
- **Remember your presenting principles.**
- **Laugh along** – Sometimes people need the visual cue that what you've said is funny. (I know, people are idiots.) And, as we know, laughter is infectious so make sure you exploit it!
- **If you're being filmed**, see the camera as an extra friend. It works really well when you come to watch it back.
- **Be prepared for audience interaction.** It's unlikely you'll get hecklers but some people like to 'get involved'. It's good to have a few witty responses in your back pocket. For example ...

    – (*If it's a free bar*) 'And that's why the free bar ends after the first drink ...'
    – (*If it's not a free bar*) 'And that's why you don't get a free bar ...'
    – 'There are some RSVPs you read with tears in your eyes.'

Post-delivery

Once you've written a good speech, you'll actually love delivering it on the day.

You might dread the thought of it today but after you've given a cracking speech, you'll be like Beyoncé coming off stage; adrenaline pumping, feeling great, desperate to take off your Spanx.

Two pieces of advice:

1   Alcohol will now go straight to your head, so take it slowly.
2   You'll be buzzing post-speech but resist the urge to talk about it for the rest of the night (though do feel free to spend every waking moment watching the video of it in the months to come).

SPEECH INSPIRATION

Gay bride speech – Delivered by Alex
Background: Alex has married Yesenia in a Humanist ceremony led by Alex's friend Amanda. The couple live in rural Indiana and met through work.

Hi everyone, thank you all so much for coming. Today is obviously such an important day for us both, and to share it with you all makes it all the more special.

We fully understand that we've dragged you into the forest in the middle of winter, but on the plus side you will get to see the hilarious sight of two famously uncoordinated people attempting to slow dance later, so every cloud, as they say.

Now, there was a time in my life where I honestly thought that I'd never find myself getting married. And truthfully, I was over the moon with it. There's nothing more I used to love than locking myself indoors and reading a book with my cat, Martin. Or, to use his full name, Martin McWhiskers the Second. Who, if I'm honest, I'd always considered my soulmate. Well, also Rihanna, but she's less easily lured into your bed with a tin of tuna and a belly rub.

Ultimately, I was happy on my own, and, not only that, dating felt hard. If you log onto Tinder in rural Indiana, you get two matches and one's likely to be a weird straight couple looking for a 'third'.

So, the dating scene felt like a no-go zone, and Martin and I were fine with that – after all, he made it very clear that other guests weren't welcome in our home when Aunt Fay stayed over for the weekend and Martin urinated in her shoes.

Then one day, with dating firmly out of my thoughts, I got an email from a new food supplier saying they were in town and hoping to meet for a chat about 'refrigeration supply chain solutions'.

Like something out of a Jane Austen book, right?

We booked a meeting a few days later, and when Yesenia arrived, she bounded into my office – read: table closest to the pastries at Starbucks – with that beaming smile and carefree attitude, and I was hooked. We spent two minutes talking about how best to keep 'bread chilled in transit' and then two hours talking about our lives, hobbies, things we love and things we don't.

As soon as she left, I couldn't stop thinking about her. I just had this feeling that 'this feels like the type of girl I could scroll through Twitter next to in bed'. So, I immediately booked a second meeting under the spurious guise of 'discussing competitive pricing structures'. Now I say that out loud, it's no wonder I was single for seven years.

Before our second meeting, I was speaking to my wonderful friend Amanda and nervously waffling – 'How will I know if she's into me?', 'I'm not even sure she's gay?' – and she just stopped me and said, 'If she likes you, she'll find some way to show you.'

Fast forward to our second meeting and Yesenia turned up in her car loudly playing 'Fast Car' by Tracy Chapman and I thought, well, *that's* a sign.

From there, there was no looking back. We hung out, we dated, we went for walks and, most importantly, when she first stayed over, Martin didn't urinate in her shoes. In fact, not only that, but it seems like Yesenia is the only other person he actually likes. Which could mean one of two things: either Martin is a good judge of character, or Yesenia and I both smell like ham.

The fact we run meat supplies companies *maybe* suggests the latter. Although what matters most is that when I'm at home, I've got my two favourites by my side, Martin and Yesenia.

To be honest, from the first few dates, I knew that being with Yesenia, there was an ease around her that I'd never experienced before. A sort of low hum of contentedness that permeated everything we did together. But I didn't expect things to move quite as quickly as they did.

We'd probably been seeing each other for a month when we went out for dinner, and Yesenia casually mentioned that the lease on her house was due to expire, and she had to find somewhere else to live. Then without even thinking, I said, 'Oh, you should come and live with me.'

I shocked myself. Normally, I wouldn't let someone even pop round for a coffee unless I'd had signed references from three acquaintances and a current employer. But it wasn't just the uncharacteristic impulsiveness that shocked me, it was also my absolute certainty that this was the right thing to do.

The feeling that this was not only a good choice, but the *only* choice. Obviously though I didn't want to seem too keen, so I quickly followed it up with a flustered, 'Just until you find somewhere else ... or whatever.'

But I was certain it was the right thing.

She moved in, and to this day still hasn't found 'somewhere else ... or whatever'. Which I *think* constitutes a win.

Everything has always been fast and instinctive with Yesenia and me. From dating to moving in together. And getting engaged was no different.

There is no huge, romantic engagement story with roses and grand gestures. We were just in bed one evening, me reading a book, her doing a crossword, and both of us feeling that low hum of contentedness. When she took my hand, placed a ring on my finger and said, 'Fancy it?'

Of course, I did. In fact, again, it felt like the only possible choice. Obviously though I didn't say that, I said (*strange crying noises*).

I think what I'm trying to get at, is how immediately perfect my time with Yesenia has always felt. Before I met her, I couldn't see a future where I wasn't on my own. And now I can't envisage a future where we're not together.

So, with that in mind, I'd like you all to join me in raising a toast to my best friend. And simply the greatest person I know: Mrs Yesenia Ortega-Miller!

SPEECH WRITTEN BY ED AMSDEN AND TOM COLES

Groom speech – Delivered by Rishaan

Background: Rishaan has married Aashi. They live in San Francisco and met online.

Good evening, everyone. Can I hear a 'Hey ya!' if you trekked all the way from Delhi this weekend? Where are my boys from Florida at? How about a 'toodle-pip' from my peeps from England? And a '*Brrrrrrr-uh!*' from my uncles and auntiyaan from the Punjab?

It means so much to us that you made such an effort to come from far and wide to be here. This is a really important day for all of us. Especially our parents. Especially *my* parents! Man, they've been waiting decades for this day to arrive. To finally be done with the burden of looking after their only son, so that I can now be someone else's problem. Sure, they had to pay a hefty dowry to make it happen. Just a solid $50,000. And a Honda Civic.

I'm kidding! Dowry? For me!? It's 2023. It was $100,000. And a BMW i4.

Dowry aside – imaginary or otherwise – this is the happiest day of my life. I never could have imagined someone like me marrying someone like Aashi. I mean, doesn't she look stunning today?

Aashi is not only incredibly beautiful, she's also achingly intelligent, razor-sharp and, above all, the boss. This is a woman who knows what she wants and I'm so glad that now includes me.

As most of you know, we met at work. Aashi was, literally, my boss.

Now I know what this sounds like: powerful, successful woman seduces young, impressionable intern. Which has a hint of truth if you count the McDonald's Happy Meals she bought me the first couple of weeks. But let me clarify – she bought them for all the team – mainly because she felt sorry about the pittance of a salary she was paying us.

Pretty quickly, I fell in love with her. She had the heart of an angel. She had the face of an angel. And just like an angel, she was way out of my league.

With each team meeting, I became more and more dumbfounded by admiration and attraction, while her respect for me went in the opposite direction. Could you blame her?

Every time she asked for my opinion on anything, my mouth would go dry, and my mind would blank with the sound of *Aaja aaa main horn payer tera* ringing in my ears. In team meetings, I'd have to stop myself imagining visions of us growing old, having children and wearing matching Christmas pyjamas.

Meanwhile, it transpires Aashi was confused about my aloof manner and was beginning to suspect I didn't appreciate having a female boss.

Now, Desi guys get a hard rep for being overbearing alpha males but, as you can see, I'm hardly alpha. I'm so far from alpha,

I'm zeta. Everyone who knows me knows I'm one of the strongest feminist allies around. Unfortunately, I'm so feminist, I don't make a move on girls I'm interested in in fear that I might offend them. And this was very much the case with Aashi. Well, that and she was a goddess.

A year went by, and I slowly worked up the courage to look Aashi in the eye occasionally. Our friendship grew and I forced myself to act cool whenever she filled me in on her dating exploits. (What? That's what happens when you don't make a move, people!)

After eight months, I handed in my notice, and at my leaving party, I went to say goodbye to her, not knowing if I'd ever see her again. Who knows if it was the four mojitos or just pure adrenaline, but I knew I had to kiss her.

And she didn't slap me. Thankfully for me, for us, for this wedding day, she wasn't offended by my move.

So here we are. I still can't believe this is happening. And I can't wait to see where we go from here: to grow old, to have children and to wear matching Christmas pyjamas with them.

Of course, whatever we do, I know one thing is for sure … Aashi will always be the boss. It might be a marriage contract rather than an employee contract that bonds us now, but rest assured, I never want to be pulled up for disciplinary behaviour.

In fact, I am going to do my utmost, for the rest of my life, to make Aashi happy. Even if it involves driving 30km to find her favourite tandoori chicken and green pepper pizza every Friday night. You know exactly where I'm talking about.

Marrying Aashi is a dream realised and it's made all the more special by all of you joining us. I'd like to thank a few special people …

Thank you to all the beautiful bridesmaids who apparently gave Aashi one heck of a send-off in New Orleans. Manhugs to my boys, the groomsmen who almost got me killed and arrested in Vegas – on consecutive days.

Finally, thank you to Aashi's parents – now *my* mum and dad – for bringing such a treasure into the world. I'll take care of her to my dying day, I promise.

Thank you also to my mother and father for being such wonderful role models and supporting me so well throughout my single years. Thank you also for welcoming Aashi to our family so warmly and for not making it immediately obvious how odd we all are. And Mum, I've already spoken to the DJ to ensure there's a 30-minute Shammi Kapoor section.

And so now, finally, it's time for the party to begin, but before you put on your dancing shoes, I would love you all to join me in a toast to my delightful wife.

(To Aashi) You are everything I want and I cannot wait to spend the rest of my life with you.

To my love, my angel, my boss and my bride: to Aashi.

WRITTEN BY SHAI HUSSAIN

Joint rhyming speech – Delivered by Selena and Ethan
Background: They live in Brisbane.

ETHAN: Ladies and gentlemen, there's so much to say.

SELENA: So we'll start with a 'thank you' for coming today.

ETHAN: It just means the world to have you all here.

SELENA: And to be in the company of those we hold dear.

ETHAN: Now, you may notice we're taking one line at a time . . .

SELENA:	And doing the whole thing as one giant rhyme ...
ETHAN:	But you know us – we're not ones to stick to tradition,
SELENA:	So here's our joint wedding speech: poem edition.
ETHAN:	When we told my brother that this was our plan, John started to doubt saying 'yes' to best man.
SELENA:	He said we were mad, but we vowed we would show him And prove young John wrong with our wedding-day poem.
ETHAN:	Let's start with a few words on our congregation, Who've travelled so far to this destination.
SELENA:	From New Zealand and Asia and Europe they've sailed, Over land, sea and air, these heroes travailed.
ETHAN:	To be here today, you've achieved a great feat!
SELENA:	Except my mum and dad, who live just down the street.

ETHAN: Truly though, thank you all for attending,
            And for all the support and love you've been
            sending.

SELENA: It hasn't been easy, planning a wedding
            With a man who doesn't know how to wash
            his own bedding . . .

ETHAN: On the flipside, Selena won't change a
            bedsheet,
            Without consulting her 'laundry and chores'
            spreadsheet.

SELENA: Between us, we make quite an opposite pair . . .

ETHAN: I mean, for starters, she still has her hair.

SELENA: And unlike me, Ethan knows how to drive.

ETHAN: I guess differences keep the attraction alive.

SELENA: But since the day we met, right back in Year
            Nine,
            I knew that this scrawny young lad would be
            mine.

ETHAN: It took me a while to think the same thing,
            But as soon as I did, I purchased a ring.

SELENA: I said yes right away, then 'What took you so
            long?'

ETHAN: And I realised I'd actually known all along.
That Selena and I were destined to be,
That I was her 'him' . . .

SELENA: . . . And I was his 'she'.

ETHAN: So, join us by raising your glasses in toast,

SELENA: To a couple who are more ambitious than most,
Who write speeches in couplets just to prove someone wrong.

ETHAN: Good job John never said, 'Bet you can't do a song.'

SELENA: Now yes, raise your glasses,

ETHAN: 'Cos we couldn't be keener . . .

SELENA: To say cheers to Ethan!

ETHAN: And cheers to Selena!

BOTH: (*Raise glasses*)

WRITTEN BY ED AMSDEN AND TOM COLES

Hello everyone, I'm so pleased to *finally* welcome you all to our
wedding. As you know, I'm not one to rush into things. It's only
taken me 12 years to finally say 'I do'. If Roisin's lucky, we might
manage to have a honeymoon at some point in the next decade. But
no promises.

I've never been the most dynamic of men. Roisin and I met
online, and it was Roisin who made the first move. In hindsight
that was a blessing. If she hadn't, I'd probably still be looking at her
profile, trying to decide whether to write something devastatingly
witty like, 'Hi, how are you?' or something more enigmatic like,
'Hello, how you doing?'

Thankfully, Roisin went with something far more
straightforward. Something along the lines of, 'How long have you
been single, and when do you want to meet for a drink?'

I found out later that whilst I'd been perusing the site on and
off for over a year, Roisin had signed up earlier that week, and had
already set up eight dates.

It seemed like this was the kind of woman I needed in my life.
Forceful, full of energy, and not put off when I turned up in a dodgy
purple shirt my housemate had convinced me was 'memorable'.
Thanks for that Steve.

We went to a restaurant of Roisin's choosing, which again was
a good thing, as my culinary knowledge at the time extended to
things I could order off a leaflet and arrived on a moped.

Back then, my career was my life. I worked late, I drank with
work colleagues, I lived with a work mate. I imagine I was, to put it
kindly, incredibly dull.

But here was this woman so full of life. With interests and hobbies and opinions. Lots and *lots* of opinions. And as I talked to her, I remembered, I had some opinions too. Many of them the complete opposite to hers, but you couldn't have everything.

We talked and laughed, and at some point she went to the bathroom and politely cancelled the bloke she was planning to go for drinks with after me.

Trying to impress her, I told her I was an expert in horse racing. I'm not sure why I thought this was impressive, and it certainly wasn't true. I'd been to the races twice, both times with work, and both times I'd been so drunk I'm not sure I even put a bet on.

But that weekend we headed off to Curragh Racecourse. And thankfully, Roisin was my good luck charm. We came home 14 euros in profit! And I even got a cheeky kiss at the train station. I was smitten.

But as we all know, the course of true love never runs completely smooth. Just six months into getting to know Roisin, she was made redundant, and had to move back with her parents whilst she decided to retrain. We had to make a decision. Were we going to call it quits, or do the long-distance thing?

Now, I knew I didn't want to lose Roisin from my life, but as a born and bred Dubliner, I also knew that the thought of going over the border every other weekend chilled me to my very core.

I, of course, learned my lesson on that one very quickly. Getting to know Roisin's friends and family so well over that time was such a gift. It turns out, just like Roisin, most of them are warm, funny and – how do I put this politely? – they really don't mince their words.

In fact, Roisin told me to burn that purple shirt before any of her family saw it, otherwise I'd never hear the last of it. And I'm pretty sure she's right.

Of course, what I really should have been worrying about was what her family would think of me. Nervous to be spending the weekend in her family home, I met Roisin straight off the train, and we headed to the pub. Then another pub. Then another pub. Then I think a kebab shop? Then I remember dancing quite enthusiastically to Justin Bieber somewhere that might have been a nightclub?

At 2am, Roisin had to wake her dad, Kenny, to carry me to bed. Not the first impression I was hoping for. Kenny, I'd like to formally apologise for that today. Although I still think you and Clodagh are partially to blame, for raising such a bad influence of a daughter.

Our two years apart made me realise just how important Roisin was in my life, so when Roisin decided to start her own business, it was actually me who suggested she move back down to Dublin, we get our own flat, and she start up her shop from there.

Thank goodness she went for it. Because two weeks after Roisin moved in, we found out she was pregnant with Jack. We were both overjoyed and overwhelmed. Turns out, setting up a cheese and wine business whilst you're pregnant is not the best of ideas.

I, of course, as a good partner, offered up my services as her personal wine taster, but apparently she didn't trust the palate of a man who thinks cheesy Tayto crisps are an appropriate dinner party hors d'oeuvre.

And she's right, of course. I have terrible taste in shirts and food and wine, and I really do like Justin Bieber. But the one thing I have excellent taste in is women. Because I knew from the moment I met Roisin she was something special. And it turns out I was right.

Just as I expected, she was a natural when it came to Jack. And when Jennifer came two years later, she managed to look after a newborn and a toddler and her business in a way that blew my mind. With fun and joy and laughter and the same determination to get things done she's had since that day she first messaged me on the dating app.

And I hope that I've helped Roisin with things too. I might be a boring bugger compared to her. I might not light up a room when I laugh, or help coach the kids' football team, or have a cocktail named after me at the local pub. But, I do love helping out Roisin with the jobs she deems boring and pointless, like stocktaking and the business accounts. And I try to keep things ticking over at home too. Not only do I always make sure there's toothpaste in both bathrooms, but I also make sure I know when there's a new series of *Ozark* on Netflix for her to binge watch.

Because there's nothing I love more than making Roisin happy. In fact, I'd like to think we make a good team. Of course, we couldn't have done it without you lot.

Steve, thanks for being my best man. Even if you did nearly ruin the whole thing with your terrible fashion advice. You were by my side right from the start and I couldn't think of anyone better to be by my side today.

To my mum and dad. Thank you for showing me what a truly loving relationship looks like. And thanks even more for all your free childcare over the past nine years. You're truly lifesavers, and we love you very much.

Kenny and Clodagh, you've raised the most amazing, beautiful, headstrong daughter, and I couldn't be more grateful. You welcomed me into the family, even after our terrible first start. If we can be half as brilliant as you are as parents, then we'll be doing a pretty good job.

Sarah, thanks for being Roisin's bridesmaid today. For someone who has so many friends, Roisin is lucky that one of the greatest of them is her sister. You're such an important part of our family, even if you are a terrible influence on the kids.

And to all of you here for coming and celebrating our marriage, we thank you all. It may have taken twelve years to get here, but honestly, I knew Roisin was the one for me on our second date, when she did a victory dance in the bar at the racecourse after we won 4 euros on a horse both ways. She was my lucky charm then, as she has been ever since.

Roisin, you look beyond gorgeous today.

Thank you for being the most amazing woman, and now my amazing wife. You've given me the best family, the most amazing home, and the most wonderful life a boring bugger like me could ever have wished for.

So, if you could all please be upstanding for the toast.

To my odds-on favourite . . . to Roisin.

SPEECH WRITTEN BY CLAIRE WETTON

Stage 5 – Over to You

This book contains a lot of advice. Take what you want and ignore the rest.

Honestly. Your speech is yours to play with.

I sincerely hope this book has given you the guidance you needed but, more importantly, I hope it has set your mind alight.

Now, it's over to you.

I've given you my most useful tips and techniques but, as the speech examples prove, you don't have to stick to my advice religiously.

There are *no* rules when it comes to creating a speech that's right for you.

All I ask is that you're brave enough to be creative and that you grab this opportunity with both hands.

In a world where we're increasingly communicating electronically, the power of a great speech has grown. Over the last decade people have rediscovered a depth and intimacy in the spoken word. It's a different type of connection and it can define your relationship with people for years to come.

Your speech has the power to leave an imprint on people's hearts. It's one of the most life-affirming gifts you can give someone; a recognition of how important they are to you.

It's also your chance to write your own story.

Have fun creating a speech that leaves your guests with a greater understanding, not only of you, but the power of love, the joy of laughter and the importance of connection.

Enjoy!

Acknowledgements

Thank you to the Speechy team for being fantastic writers who constantly delight me with their wit and dedication to our little speechwriting revolution.

Ed, Tom, Claire, Stuart, Andrew, Gemma, Shai and James; thank you for being creative geniuses and lovely people to boot.

Gemma Waldron, thank you for being the first person I trusted to read the book. You are the apostrophe queen and a valued friend.

Thank you to my 'other' team. Roger, Senen, Ingo, my wonderful mum, Anne, and all my awesome family and friends (you know who you are!) for helping me understand what love really means and live a life filled with humour.

A special thank-you to Roger for asking me to marry you and, consequently, giving me an opportunity to give a bride speech. Thank you for all the support you've given me whilst setting up Speechy and writing this book. I owe you some serious 'bench time'.

Thank you to my agent, Clare Grist Taylor, who immediately recognised why 'another' wedding speech guide was needed, and Tom Asker, my editor at Little, Brown, for also instantly getting it.

Thank you to all the other clever folk at Little, Brown who have contributed to making this book what it is, including Ben McConnell, Matt Burne and Ella Garrett.

Thank you to all the clever, inspiring influencers and experts who have been quoted and offered their wisdom and insights so willingly. I'm honoured to include your words in the book.

Thank you to all the incredible grooms and brides I've been lucky enough to work with over the last seven years and all the people who have trusted me to write their wedding speech. It's been fun, educational and an absolute honour.

Finally, thank *you* for choosing to read this book.

I hope it has made you excited about the prospect of giving a speech rather than daunted by it. I hope you've enjoyed finding the storyteller lurking within. And I also hope it's helped you notice all the delightful quirks that make your relationship as wonderful as it is.

Here's to love...

PS – Please let me know how your speech goes. I'm stupidly nosey. You can get in touch with me at heidi@speechy.com

And if you enjoyed reading the book, please do leave an online review.

It really helps spread the word and, hopefully, might help other nearlyweds in need.

YOUR SPEECH SCRIBBLES

YOUR SPEECH SCRIBBLES

YOUR SPEECH SCRIBBLES

YOUR SPEECH SCRIBBLES

YOUR SPEECH SCRIBBLES

YOUR SPEECH SCRIBBLES

YOUR SPEECH SCRIBBLES

IF YOU'RE LOOKING FOR FURTHER HELP AND
GUIDANCE ON THE BIG DAY, CHECK OUT THE
OTHER TITLES AVAILABLE FROM US OVERLEAF . . .

A-Z Of Wedding Wisdom: Expert Advice on Planning Your Wedding
SUZAN ST MAUR

Planning and organising your wedding is quite a challenge, especially for today's busy brides and grooms. The good news is that many people have been there, done it and got the T-shirt. Sharing their experience can save you a vast amount of time, money, energy and sanity when it comes to your own Big Day. In this book Suzan St Maur has gathered together many years' worth of wedding wisdom from wedding planners, wedding suppliers, and married folks themselves: experiences, expert advice, shortcuts, tips, and much more. No matter how complex your wedding is going to be, the advice you'll find in this book is priceless. In easy-to-read, easy-to-reference encyclopaedic style, Suzan covers all the usual – and the more unusual – issues you may have to deal with when planning your wedding.

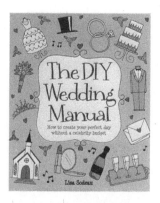

The DIY Wedding Manual
LISA SODEAU

This book will show you that with a little bit of planning and preparation, it is possible to have the day of your dreams without starting married life in debt. The average cost of a wedding is about as much as a deposit on a house, but one thing the 'credit crunch' taught us all is that there are many areas in our lives where we can save money by doing things ourselves. So why should weddings be an exception? Whether it's boom or bust you don't have to spend a fortune. You really can create your own special day by doing it yourself and having fun along the way. This book is packed with top tips and money saving ideas for: Stationery, Venues, Flowers, Transport, Hair and Make-up, Photographs, Food and Drink, the Reception and much more – including tips from live brides and over 100 budget busting ideas.

Planning A Winter Wedding: And How to Do it in Style
SUZAN ST MAUR

Weddings in the cooler months of the year can offer huge cost savings, afford spectacular locations and travel opportunities, and are more reliably planned for when you are not hoping for the appearance of the sun. With themes ranging from autumn leaves to winter wonderlands and mid-winter festivals, cooler-month weddings can be particularly romantic, glamorous, beautiful and unusual. Weddings expert Suzan St Maur shows you how to: pick a superb location at a far lower price than in peak season; create a magical, themed small wedding; arrange a wedding abroad that's breath-taking value for money; organise fun hen and stag parties at bargain prices; choose a truly charming theme you'll cherish forever; select outfits that make a striking fashion statement; fire up your imagination with seasonal floral and other lovely decorations; savour the appetising delights of cooler-months food and drinks; and, find and book a honeymoon to suit your tastes as well as your wallet.

The Little Book of Humanist Weddings: Enduring inspiration for celebrating love and commitment
ANDREW COPSON & ALICE ROBERTS

From the authors of the *Sunday Times* bestseller *The Little Book of Humanism.*

A humanist wedding ceremony allows couples the freedom to express their love in a completely personal way – and choose what marriage means to them.

In a beautiful collection of insights from humanist celebrants, plus quotes, poems and meditations from humanist writers and thinkers throughout history, *The Little Book of Humanist Weddings* is filled with inspiration to complement your unique celebration of love and commitment.